History
and
Power of Mind

RICHARD INGALESE

COSIMOCLASSICS

NEW YORK

History and Power of Mind
Cover © 2007 Cosimo, Inc.

For information, address:

Cosimo, P.O. Box 416
Old Chelsea Station
New York, NY 10113-0416

or visit our website at:
www.cosimobooks.com

History and Power of Mind was originally published in 1902.

Cover design by www.kerndesign.net

ISBN: 978-1-60206-329-7

Before we take up the study of the emotional nature and its colors, it may be well to examine that force which built man's physical form, and which builds all physical forms——the force we call "life."

——from Lecture VI, "Colors of Thought Vibration"

PREFACE

THIS book is made up from personal notes and stenographic reports of lectures delivered in New York City during the seasons of 1900-1901-1902, with the addition of some new matter in the form of amplifications. The compilation is made at the request of my students and is published primarily for their benefit. The material is left in the form in which it was delivered.

The book may not appeal to the orthodox religionist nor to the materialist; but may prove interesting, if not enlightening, to the agnostic and to the investigator of either psychic phenomena, or the phenomena of mental therapeutics.

The modern teachings of the Science of Mind have not appealed to many thinkers because of the vagueness of thought and expression of the majority of those who attempt to present them; and also because of the lack of a working hypothesis needed to explain the law under which both psychic and mental phenomena occur. This book is an attempt toward supplying the latter deficiency by stating laws under which Mind evolves and operates.

The author does not claim any original research or discoveries along these lines, having had the matter herein contained given to him in the course of his study, under trained minds who had verified these facts for themselves and who required him to do the same.

The Occult forces of nature and their modes of manifestation have been known for ages to certain secret orders which have not deemed it wise heretofore to give their knowledge to the world. This age, however, seems, in their judgment, propitious for the wider spread of such knowledge both because many independent investigators are discovering for themselves something about these forces and, in their ignorance, are perverting the use of them—as witness hypnotism —and because the advanced men of the race have reached a point where they are desirous of this knowledge, and every mental demand brings its supply.

"The History and Power of Mind," was selected for a title because the history of mind is the history of man; and these lectures first trace mind's, or psychic man's, origin and development, and then describe the power of mind and its modes of manifestation.

It may not be amiss to state in conclusion that the book is not written for the purpose of propagandism. Something of the operation of Nature's

Laws is described in these lectures, and the acceptance or rejection of the statements made will not change the Laws nor affect the author.

R. I.

New York City, October 1st, 1902.

RETROSPECTION AND FORECAST

THE taking over of our books by Dodd, Mead & Company gives me an opportunity to revise this volume and to correct many verbal errors, some of them serious, which crept into, or were overlooked in former editions. In the two decades which have elapsed since first these teachings were given to the World my studies have continued and have been broadened; but I find nothing of a basic nature to revise in this book. Of course much could be added, but such knowledge as is permissible to be given out will be issued later in a separate volume.*

I have received many hundreds of letters during the period stated, asking for elucidation on various points covered by the text. Most of these could have been self-answered if the writers had studied the text more carefully, or had read the two supplemental books * belonging to the series. But the constant recurrence of the same questions in so many letters has made it advisable to offer a few explanations which may prevent uncertainty in the minds of present or future readers.

Much perplexity has arisen over the subject of the "Period of Evolution," briefly sketched in

---

* The philosophic series now consist of the following books: "The History and Power of Mind," "Occult Philosophy," "Fragments of Truth" and "The Greater Mysteries."

Chapter I, and more lightly touched upon elsewhere. This has been particularly true of readers who have studied the semi-esoteric teachings of modern Theosophy, of Astrology and of Oriental literature. The esoteric facts are these: Occultism commences to compute Periods of Evolution from the beginning of the next Solar Cycle after the stream of *in*volution had brought the last of the human Egos or Minds from a previous planet to this Earth.

Now, as modern Astronomy correctly states, it takes the Sun something over twenty-five thousand years to complete its circuit through the Zodiacal signs, and this period of time is called a solar cycle. In occult or semi-occult literature a solar cycle is designated as an "Age of the Earth," a "Period of Mundane Evolution," or "Race Period." There are seven such Sun Cycles or Periods of activity in which man may evolve on this planet. These Sun Cycles are divided into twelve sub-cycles or periods, each consisting of about two thousand years, or the length of time it takes for the Sun to pass from one sign of the Zodiac to another.

In Oriental literature these are called " Sub-Race Periods," and they are also known, among Occultists, as a "Nation's Age," for it is during such a period that a Nation is born, matures, grows old and dies. It is interesting to verify this fact in history, especially in contemporaneous history, for the leading Nations of Europe are now ending their two thousand year cycle.

This, in a measure, answers the questions so often asked, ''Have we finished the Sun Cycle of Pisces and are we in the Aquarian Age?'' To both questions the Occultist would answer, No. We are now concluding the Age of Pisces and hence the disturbances in every line of human endeavor.

At the end of each Sub-Cycle and peculiarly at the end of each Solar Cycle, a re-adjustment in men's affairs and in the Earth takes place. Those are the days of Judgment for that Period or Cycle, and it was in reference to the end of the Piscean Age that the Nazarene Occultist gave the prophecy concerning the ''end of the World,'' as the King James version has it, or the ''Consummation of the Age,'' as the revised version of the New Testament puts it.

Connecting the two thousand year cycles are minor cycles, overlapping in an evolutionary sense the cycles they connect, as a link in a chain. And it is in these connecting, smaller cycles that the re-adjustments take place.

The writers of the letters referred to repeatedly asked, ''How can you continue to assert that there is an exact Law of Justice, as you do throughout the book, when all around us we see so much injustice?''

The answer is plain—as a man usually pays as he goes, but monthly or yearly settles all outstanding accounts, so evolving man usually sows and reaps in the same life, but outstanding, evolutionary debts are settled in full during the minor Cycles which connect the major ones.

For a concrete example we will take the thirty years commencing with 1895 and lasting through 1925. That Period constitutes an overlapping Cycle of Compensation. During that time all World, National, Community and Individual wrongs must be righted. It is the harvest time for men's thoughts and acts.

Necessarily undeveloped man has not sown wisely and hence the chaos into which we are rapidly whirling. But all evil must be swept away before man can commence a new Cycle of Evolution. It is a sub-conscious reminiscence of the beginning of a new Major Cycle that has led man to dream of Arcadias and to prophesy millenniums, for only the good endures.

Prior to 1900 and before the Custodians of Occult knowledge gave permission to reveal, in these lectures, esoteric truths, the World had never heard of the colors of thought vibration, of Cosmic Forces and their colors, of the vibratory color of man's aura and its connection with Cosmic Forces, nor of the practical use of such knowledge.

When the World first heard of these matters it was incredulous, and even students were in doubt, but time, which proves all things, has justified the claims of the Occultist and has shown that all mental phenomena of the modern cults are founded upon the vibratory theories of mind and matter herein set forth. And now, on every side, among thinking people and among those who pretend to think, these heretofore esoteric matters are discussed as common knowledge and too often are carried to absurd extremes by those who least understand them.

A careful study of this book, and particularly of Chapters VI, X and XI, will open new avenues of knowledge and show the way to spiritual development in the true and Occult sense—meaning the development in man of the attributes of the Spirit—of God, which are Omniscience, Omnipotence and Omnipresence. As man raises his vibrations and draws the higher Cosmic Forces into his mind and body, his knowledge, force and consciousness expand and he grows more godlike, until at length, in the fruition of time, he becomes a god.

Too much stress cannot be laid upon this subject, for, after all, our evolutionary aim is to become something better than we are. One should not deprecate, in any manner, man's attempt to better his social, financial or intellectual condition, but man should know that these are all but means to an end—soul growth.

The struggle engendered by man in carrying out his material ambitions gives him courage, perseverance, patience and strength, also experience which ripens into knowledge. Thus is character built, the nature of which is dependent upon the means used by him. One who recognizes that his vocation is but a method of growth ceases to feel any burden in his work and enjoys the conflict and the conquest equally. 'To such a one there is no gradation of labor nor degradation in service.

By this is not meant that all labor is equal commercially, but is equally noble if used as a means to an end, and, as such, is well done—and in the New Era, after 1925, only the drones—if any are left—will be without honor.

Most earnestly is it recommended to each reader to peruse—not cursorily read—Chapter VIII dealing with psychic phenomena. The World War, with its necessary attendant famine and plagues, has swept out of physical manifestation millions of egos, many of whom carried with them hatred of those left behind. Hatred begets a desire for revenge, a primitive but powerful instinct. 'The medium, to gratify this impulse of excarnated egos, is necessarily limited to psychic instrumentalities, and herein lie the intensified dangers enumerated in the Chapter in question.

It is not at all surprising that a psychic wave is sweeping around the Earth at the present time and that tons of books are being weekly turned off the press to supply information and misinformation concerning the future state of man.

Priesthood has ever held out hope to the bereaved ones left behind; but braver souls, feeling doubt corroding their creeds, have sought from age to age to prove for themselves the persistency of the personality after physical death. So general is this impulse at the present time that modern necromancy has become a parlor pastime, when it is not an effort of love to reach a dear but unwilling pioneer upon the subjective side of life.

Every Occultist willingly concedes that mind is the master of matter and persists after the material form has disappeared. It is also conceded that in many instances the communicating excarnated ego is the one whose identity is claimed. But this does not change the sad fact that more often the identity cannot be established and that impersonation is practiced to the detriment of the investigator. There is no certainty in psychic inquiry unless the investigator is himself an independent clairvoyant, and then there is but little safety for him unless he has learned to permanently remain positive or to protect himself with Cosmic Forces.

Many inquirers have erroneously concluded that, since all disease has its origin in a mental cause, only mind can cure; and therefore refuse all material aid in sickness. This is not necessarily a logical nor a wise conclusion. The mental cause may have ceased to operate after the physical manifestation, and in such a case proper material remedies would bring about chemical and physical changes for the better. If the mental cause still persists, then both mind and medicine must be used. It is always safer at this stage of our development to use mental and Cosmic Forces as well as the natural remedies which a kindly Providence has provided. This is not meant as recommendatory of mineral drugs, poisons and serums, such as are too frequently used by some practitioners of the present day. But, by natural remedies, are meant the various drugless systems, diet, hygiene and herbs. Nature has provided in most localities herbal remedies for the diseases most likely to be generated in those localities, and it is man's privilege to study nature and to learn to work with her in preserving the physical body so that, in and through it, he may more highly evolve.

It stands to reason that if a man can preserve

his body, as an efficient instrument, for a longer period than is the present average age of men, he has thereby the greater advantage in the evolutionary race.

For ages an Occult School of medicine has existed in which the few accepted students are taught the vibratory rate and chemical action of grasses, roots, herbs and trees, and particularly the oils and quintessences derived therefrom.

But by far the greatest number of inquiries received in all these years pertained to Chapter XII. So many quaint, queer and pathetic letters were written about the Law of Opulence that sometimes one wondered if the other parts of the book were often read. The teachings were intended to supply the demands that earnest hearts had made along Spiritual, mental and material lines. It was natural to suppose that the great majority of readers would prefer to have rather than to be; but one was scarcely prepared to find that eighty per cent of all inquiries were concerning material possessions. This was compensated for, in a measure, by those letters which told of the conquest of self.

Many students, by study and experimentation, gained a comprehension of the Law of Attraction and used it successfully along all lines. Many more persons, however, told of failure, but the letters written clearly revealed the reason—the writers had failed to understand either the text or themselves. So many persons had day-dreamed, thinking that they were creating and concentrating. Others who had never earned more than one or two hundred dollars a month, and were working eight hours a day for that amount, were disappointed because their mental work of fifteen minutes a day for a few months had not brought independent wealth.

The majority of the letters showed that vanity had been the obstruction to success. Persons who had never before heard of the power of mind, upon reading the book, determined that hence-forth they would cease to work physically and would use mind exclusively. They concluded that they were able to dispense with all centers through which to work—all occupations—and, not having the requisite knowledge and experience with the Law, and lacking in their power of concentration, naturally they failed.

The attention of readers is again called to the fact that most of us belong to the class designated as "Physico-mental workers," and that it takes time, effort and experience to remove ourselves from this class.

The Law of Attraction is the source from which we receive; but we must do more than sit at our desks and demand money, travel, good times and nothing to do. We will find that all who have succeeded have had an occupation, a center, in the beginning, which grew enormously under the application of the Law of Demand.

To acquire wealth, be it soul wealth or material wealth, one must possess desire, determination and the power of concentration. And it is according to the degree in which one possesses these three attributes of mind that one succeeds. It is so important to realize this fact that a repetition of it, in a slightly different form, may be excused, for it embodies the general principles which bring success.

To use the Law of Attraction successfully, therefore, one should:

First. Desire intently to possess a thing or quality.

Second. Determine, or will to possess it.

Third. Concentrate all mental *and* physical effort to acquire possession. This is mental efficiency.

Never yield to disappointment, for that is a counter force to the Creative. Never stop working to attain your object, but keep persistently at it until success crowns your efforts. By so doing you create a condition which cannot be ignored by men or by Law; for a pathway of invisible, magnetic cords stronger than steel is created between you and your object—if you choose to make it so by your power of Concentration.

Never give up working because results do not come when you desire or expect them. Discouragement, disappointment, anger, impatience and doubt in your power to succeed are the only things that can delay or prevent the consummation of your hopes and desires.   R. I.

Los Angeles, California,
        February, 1920.

CONTENTS

THE HISTORY AND POWER OF MIND

LECTURE ONE

OCCULTISM, ITS PAST, PRESENT AND FUTURE

To many persons the subjects discussed in these lectures may appear preposterous, and therefore those of you who have not studied along metaphysical lines are requested to hold yourselves agnostically until this entire course shall be finished. You do not know whether Occultism is true or not; you are now ready to examine the subject and, after having heard the entire exposition, you will be in a position to judge whether it offers a logical, working hypothesis, and whether it is worthy to receive more of your time and consideration. If it is true it can be demonstrated, for truth is always demonstrable. You can prove by demonstration each of the fundamental statements that will be made, as you can prove a proposition in mathematics. When I say truth is demonstrable, do not understand me to mean that it is capable of being demonstrated immediately upon hearing it. Everything must unfold. You cannot raise your body on a horizontal bar the first time you try because your muscles are not strong enough; but after your muscles have become strengthened by practice you may be capable of raising your body to any position you desire. So it is with a person who has never used his mind in scientific reasoning or in concentration. He should not flatter himself that he can immediately accomplish what a person who has practiced for many years can do. If you use your mind along the lines indicated in these lectures you will find that there will be a continuous growth for you, and that the time will come when you can do anything that you desire. A very large promise, you may say, but if it is true I assure you it is demonstrable.

Our first subject is "Occultism, Its Past, Present and Future." This is an introductory lecture, giving something of the history of Occultism and of the Occultists in order that we may know the source from which our information is derived.

The Century Dictionary gives the definition of Occultism as: "The doctrine, practice or rites of things occult or mysterious; the Occult Sciences or their study; mysticism; esotericism." In the Middle Ages Occult Science or Occultism embraced primarily what is now known as the physi-

cal sciences. It was understood to mean those
things which were unknown, but which by experimentation might become known. Chemistry, as a
branch of Alchemy, was regarded as one of the
Occult Sciences because it was largely unknown,
but through investigation and experimentation it
constantly became better known. But Occultism
also had a secondary meaning which was coupled
with the first, namely, mysticism, esotericism.
In ancient days people thought it not unwise to
attempt the discovery of the unknown through
experimentation with the subjective as well as the
objective side of nature, and the two meanings,
that which pertained to the objective, which was
unknown but could be ascertained, and that which
pertained to the subjective, which was unknown
but could be ascertained, were both included in the
term Occultism.

Materialism as it grew in strength called the
unknown (which was becoming known on the objective or visible side of life) "Science," but
stamped the belief in or the investigation of the
subjective side of life as "superstition." And
most people became very much afraid of that
word, and became afraid of being known as super-
stitious even more than to be known as ignorant;
and such persons preferred to remain ignorant
of the Occult. In time the word Occultism grew
to mean that which pertained to the subjective—

that which pertained to esotericism, and at present it is defined as esotericism.

As you go back in history you will find that esotericism has everywhere played a large part in moulding the thoughts of men. There were always the esoteric and the exoteric religions and sciences. There always has been and there will be for ages yet to come one religion for the masses and another for the students. There have been for a long time, and for some time yet to come there will be two sciences—one for the materialist, diluted for the masses, and another for the students of Occultism. You will find traces of this duality in any religion at any period in history. The Nazarene, the inspired leader of the Christians, after having taught the multitude in parables and having withdrawn to one side, was questioned by His disciples: "Why speakest thou to them in parables?" He answered: "Because it is given unto you to know the mysteries of the kingdom of heaven, but to them it is not given." And afterward He unfolded to His disciples the esoteric side of His teachings, thus giving them truths that were not for the masses. And in all religions, whether it be the Egyptian, Buddhism, or that precursor of the Christian religion— Judaism, there are truths which are revealed only to the student. In Judaism there was the Jehovic teaching for the masses, the Cabalistic for the most secret students, and between these two was a third, the Talmudic, which partook of the nature of both. So the truth reached all grades of society according to the comprehension of each—a plan that was adopted later by the Church of Rome with very great success.

Of course many religionists, especially those calling themselves Christians, will deny that there is any esotericism in their faith. But those who are acquainted with the history of the early Christian Church and the writings of the Fathers, and those who are familiar with the philosophy of The Logos, and the mysticism of Paul as shown in his Epistles, will never attempt to deny it to the educated.

But however violent the denial of esotericism may be by the religionist, it will not exceed in violence the denial of the term "science" to anything pertaining to the occult by the majority of the modern physicists; yet scorn, laughter or denial will not blot from the pages of either sacred or profane history the fact that Magic was and is practiced among all people. The existence of magic necessitates the knowledge of certain laws and forces which are as yet unknown to the materialist, though modern science, having gone almost to the limit of the visible, is now beginning to knock at the door of the Occult Sciences and to pry into the invisible. It is already studying the ether, ions, electrical invisibles, atoms and radiant matter. It is only a few weeks since Flammarion, in one of his articles, said that he was a student of Occultism, and that henceforth all progressive men of science would have to study along that line.

According to the teachings of esotericism Occultism is the science of Divine Unfoldment. The student of Occultism regards Deity as the All; and is taught that there is not nor cannot be any manifestation outside of Deity. Whether we look at a blade of grass, or a drop of water, or upon our planet with its teeming myriads of men and animals, or look away into space at system after system of worlds, all is Deity in various states of manifestation. The Occultist is primarily an evolutionist and says that all evolution is carried on during vast periods of time, which he calls Cosmic Days; that Deity idealizes a picture of what It will accomplish during a Cosmic Day, and then the whole impulse of evolution—which is Divine Energy or Impulse—is onward and upward, striving ever to reach that idealization.

Everything in the universe is an unfoldment of Deity Itself, and Occultism is the science of that Unfoldment. It teaches the laws under which that Unfoldment takes place, not only upon the objective plane of life but also upon the subjective plane. The Occultist finds that where he merely

studies the modern sciences he is only studying
the sciences of effects, for there is not one of the
modern sciences that teaches the cause of phenomena. Take the subject where modern science
has perhaps made as much progress as in any
other line—embryology. We find there is a germ;
it has a form of life; a method of accretion; it
reaches a certain point of development; then ask
a scientific man what it is going to be, a fish, a
bird, a reptile or a man, and he cannot answer.
Up to this point the formation of a germ of each
kind is identical with the others. But after this
point has been reached there is new accretion, a
new form is assumed, and the germ may become
a bird, a fish, a reptile or a man; but the form
that it takes was indelibly stamped upon it from
the beginning. How was it stamped? What determines the diverging point, what determines
the form of consciousness, the form of expression?
In the science of embryology there is no satisfac-
tory answer to be had because here, as you see,
is the study of effects. The cause is not looked
for, is not found.

The student of Occultism says, I want to know
when the ideal which determined all its future
growth was stamped upon that germ. I want to
know why, when it reached that point, it became
a man instead of a bird; why it drew to itself
certain elements and threw off others. I want to

know the laws that govern the subjective side of life; I want the veil to be torn away, that I may see the cause of form, and not only its effects. This is why he attempts to study first upon the objective side of life and then upon the subjective, or to study them contemporaneously.

As materialistic as was the Nineteenth Century, we find that a few men once more began to turn their thoughts toward the realm of the unknown and unseen in order to discover, if possible, the "why" of existence. And certain scientific men thought it not unreasonable nor undignified to investigate the Occult or to organize The Society for Psychical Research for the purpose of investigating these occult subjects. We have seen the great cult of Spiritualism spreading through the world and have witnessed the revival of Palmistry and of Astrology and other quasi Occult Sciences. Then following these, the crowning effort of all, we find that a great psychic wave swept over the world and man began to realize that he was Mind and as such was neither bound by time nor by space, but could send his thoughts in any given direction and could communicate without words with distant minds; and that mind could compel matter to obey it. With the awakening of the world the Occult Sciences have again challenged the attention of the most progressive men of the race.

But man grows tired of externals and life after life as he evolves he studies deeper and deeper into Nature's laws. We do not always accomplish the same amount of study in each life because we think we have not the time for study. We believe we have so much else to do that is of much more importance to us. Then there is the external world with its duties and pleasures and our attention is so deeply engaged with these things that we have no time left for more serious subjects. But in each life we take up as much of the study of these sciences as we have the time and inclination for, and gradually after many ages have passed we become earnest and devoted students.

A knowledge of Occult Law may be gained in two ways, by original research and by teachers. There are courageous souls who choose to progress along the lines of personal experimentation instead of taking the easier and perhaps the better way of gaining a knowledge of its principles through the aid of teachers. These strong souls often make terrible mistakes and unnecessary sacrifices, for, after leaving the objective plane, they come upon the hidden or subjective side where there are forces and agencies that turn to naught man's thought and efforts unless both be properly directed. But even when knowledge has been gained through teachers it does not put an end to experimentation; because the teacher explains the law and leaves the pupil to make his own verification after having been taught how it should be done. The knowledge comes, however, as all real knowledge must, by experimentation and by experience.

Who are the teachers? They may be grouped into three great classes, Masters, Adepts and Students. The Masters of Occultism are those who, in a prior period of Cosmic evolution, passed upward through the human stage until they reached the Divine, and became Gods. When a new Cosmic Day commences, and new planets are formed, and men are brought into existence for the purpose of unfolding more and more of the Deity within themselves and enlarging their consciousness as individualized parts of nature, the Masters are they who lead and teach the evolving race. The Adepts are those advanced men of our race who are students of the Masters, while at the same time they are teachers of their less developed brothers. They are men who have perfected themselves along certain lines, but have not reached perfection along all lines. The Students are they who are studying under these Adepts; they are persons who desire to know the truth, and have devoted themselves to the study of these particular sciences. They hold the same relation to the Adepts as the Adepts hold to the Masters.

There are different grades of Masters because they who finished their evolution upon their system of worlds earlier in the great Cosmic Day are stronger than they who finished later. And so there are grades of Adepts and of Students. We find that there are everywhere grades of intelligence. In other words, that which Huxley speaks of as a scientific necessity is true, and there are intelligences in this Universe as superior to man as man is superior to a black beetle. Take, for instance, a Patagonian or an Australian Bushman, and contrast him with an Emerson. What a vast gulf separates these two intelligences! Yet both are proceeding upward in their evolutionary career; the one, of course, being in advance of the other.

And it does not require much scientific imagination to conceive that there is an infinite gradation of intelligence because we see such a diversity everywhere. Then it is only logical to suppose that what is true upon the lower plane of our daily experience is also true throughout nature.

The Masters and Adepts are the custodians of the Occult Sciences, which are perfected sciences, it is claimed, because they cover all departments of nature, both physical and metaphysical, the objective and the subjective.

Now, all the facts and principles of these sciences must be verified by each person as he progresses along his evolutionary path. I may tell you something that may seem absurd to you; or you may say "that sounds reasonable," and therefore you believe it. I may tell you something else, and you say, "I believe that is true because both the intuitive and rational portions of my nature endorse it." But you do not *know* whether it is true or not. In the first case you have a disbelief, in the next two cases a belief; but before you have a knowledge, you must verify the truth of my assertion. And so it is that every student of Occultism must verify each statement of his teacher in order that he may make it a part of his own being—that he may know that it is true; otherwise it would be only a belief, and beliefs do not amount to much, because there are almost as many beliefs and theories as there are individuals.

In this Cosmic Day Occultism commenced when the Masters came upon this planet to teach mankind. The evolution on this planet is divided into a certain number of periods, and we are at the present time in what the Occultists know as the fifth period. In the first and second periods very little was accomplished by man. He was, as it were, in a new world with new sensations and new experiences, and his life was entirely objective, and largely animal. His theater of activity was that continent known to tradition as "The Land of the Gods," "Mount Muru," "The Imperishable Isles," or what we would prosaically call the "Continent of the North Pole."

During the third period of evolution, man lived upon the continent known as Lemuria—a continent lying in the Pacific Ocean, Arabian Sea and Indian Ocean. Its Northern portion was much in the present location of Australia, the Philippines, and the Islands of the Southern Pacific; all of which constitute the remnants of that continent now sunken beneath the seas. That periods occur in which there is a sinking of certain continents, and a rising of others, is as well known to Physicists as to Occultists. In Lemuria man passed from his lowest state of animal existence into what we may call a more rational or human state. His development during this time is substantially shown in the history of primitive man. Some of the egos, outstripping the others, succeeded in reaching adeptship along certain lines, but the great mass of the people lived sensuous and sensual lives. There was very little spirituality manifested by the race during this period, and the perversion of natural laws and forces became marked toward its close.

The most notable event which occurred on that continent, immediately prior to the cataclysm which swept it beneath the waters, was the establishment of colonies in India. The colonists con-

sisted of Masters, the Adepts and the cream of
the race. It was these colonists who built the
rock temples of Elephanta and the other great
temples of India—those temples in which mysticism seems to have had its earlier home; and
where, upon their walls, are painted the strange
old symbols, in colors, that indicate the history
and the growth of man.

Those were the souls who gave to India its
riches in literature and philosophy, and established the mighty empires which even tradition
has forgotten. But it was the degenerate descendants of these colonists who spread Northward and
Westward, and populated first Asia, and later,
Europe.

After the continent of Lemuria had passed
away, then came the fourth period, with man's
field of activity in Atlantis. Atlantis extended
from the West Indies to the coast of Central and
Northern Africa, as we know from the investigations of the British Government, which spent
many years, and large sums of money, in deter-
mining the extent of the sunken continent; and it
was here that civilization proceeded with tremendous strides. All the accumulated knowledge
of the other periods was stored in the minds of
those who had been the Lemurians, and were then
incarnating as Atlanteans. As they acquired
greater and greater knowledge, they not only

reached a point in mechanical development almost as great as our own, but they also took up the study of Occultism, which became common among the people.

By that time the great Masters had retired from physical contact with men, and the Adepts had taken their places as direct teachers of the people. They moved among men, and were the kings and rulers, the law-givers and inventors; in fact, they were the inspirers of the race up to the time it reached its highest point of development in that period.

Then the continent became divided into five great kingdoms, and in each of these there were lodges of Adepts. At the height of Atlantis' glory, once more the people turned to sensual abandonment, and the Adepts withdrew into Retreats with their pupils, for the people refused to listen to them, or to be aided by them any longer. In the course of time, materialism swept over that continent, as it has swept over Europe and America; and Occultism was forgotten by the masses, and remembered only by the few; and then, gradually, that which was pure Occultism became perverted, and men began to use their powers criminally. Those who remembered or practiced Occultism, put into operation mental and certain other forces which enslaved all those who had forgotten how to use their own forces, or who were not developed to the same point as themselves. And thus Atlantis became a continent where a few immensely wealthy, powerful and strong egos ruled the majority of the people, and made them their slaves.

But the misuse of Occult forces brought its re-action, as it always does, and, as Plato tells us, Atlantis suddenly became submerged. You remember that when he went to Egypt he was informed that the last remnants of Atlantis had disappeared about five thousand years prior to his visit; and also that the priests had records of the old continent, as well as of their own country, which extended back thousands of years. These records were kept by the Occultists who were priests in the time of Plato, and are still kept in triplicate; one copy has been placed in each of the three great repositories situated on separate continents.

Before Atlantis went down those of the inhabitants who had preserved their purity and who were trying to lead upright lives, were taken by the Adepts out of the country. Those living in the Western Empires were colonized in Central and South America. In Central America that rare civilization which preceded our own was founded, and was the duplicate in every respect of the one formerly established in India. The degenerate descendants from the Central American civilization emigrated to North and South America and populated them. The degeneracy of these aboriginal Americans was due to the fact that at this time in that Fourth Period the undeveloped souls of the Atlanteans were incarnating in those bodies; for it was with the Atlanteans as it had been with the Lemurians, the strongest souls came first and became the pioneers. They bore the heaviest burdens and thus prepared the way for the less developed souls who had not the strength to do the work that their elder brothers had done. And it should not be forgotten that the history of the Lemurians and the Atlanteans is but the history of ourselves. Our strongest and bravest souls came forward to start the Fifth Period onward in its evolution, as even a cursory reading of general history will disclose, and they have reappeared from time to time to manifest their energies in the several lines of human achievement, in order to teach, help and direct the course of events.

From the Eastern Empires of Atlantis the advanced souls went into Africa and laid the foundation of what is known now as the Egyptian Empire. And this brings us to the Fifth Period, in which Occultism was again taught popularly and openly among the people. A study of Egyptian history reveals that during its entire period there were Occultists—Magicians they were called—who could produce great phenomena. They were teachers of the people and were the priests and law-givers; they were the friends of kings and were consulted whenever there was sickness or national calamity. These teachers were the Adepts who came in contact with the people.

In the Fifth Period, which is the present one, the descendants of the colony which remained in India, having reached the height of its prosperity and development, passed Westward and founded the Assyrian and Babylonian Empires. There again the Adepts moved among men. In both sacred and profane history of those times we find that the Magi were able to cure all manner of diseases and to manipulate the laws of nature. Passing upward from Babylon and Syria to the Mediterranean on the one side and through Egypt to the Mediterranean on the other, we find that the great remnants of the Third and Fourth Periods were merged and blended in the Fifth Period in the Phœnician, the Grecian, the Carthaginian and the Roman peoples.

This is not a statement of occult history in full; but is merely the barest outline in order to show you how Occultism has been presented in the past, and how it has been preserved for us.

At the beginning of this Fifth Period we had a new burst of occult knowledge and force, because all the knowledge acquired in the preceding periods by the egos had been brought over in these later incarnations, and in the early history of each of the Nations mentioned Occultism was taught to the people once more. The Adepts were friends of the people and were freely consulted by them. But gradually as materialism advanced and sensuality became the dominant trait of each of these peoples, the Adepts withdrew again from personal contact with the world—as the great Masters had withdrawn in previous periods of time.

In Greece materialism in its most artistic form began to stamp itself upon the minds of the people, who turned from spiritual teachings and caused the Adepts to withdraw entirely from the world. And it came to pass that all magic or Occultism, for they were identical in those days, was confined to what is known now as temple magic and was practiced by the priests who were students of the Adepts. In various Grecian temples mechanical or ceremonial magic was taught; that is, a knowledge of mental forces united with a knowledge of chemistry and alchemy, by the blending of which great phenomena were produced. Some record of this great knowledge is preserved even in the histories which you have.

Before Occultism in Greece passed away one final attempt was made to counteract materialism, and the Eleusinian Mysteries were founded. In these mysteries the development and evolution of the human soul were taught in symbolic form and the wisest men of that age thought it a privilege to be initiated into these Mysteries. But even this proved unavailing to stem the tide of materialism and therefore the priests ceased to publicly proclaim or exert their occult powers. Occasionally some enthusiastic student came forward and exhibited his knowledge of the Occult by the performance of a few miracles and marvelous phenomena; but the people as a whole were too materialistic to be taught anything better or higher than their own gross beliefs and soon such students had to retire from public work.

Then Christianity arose, and its doctrines were received by a great many who, after a brief period of genuine revival of spirituality, used them for political purposes. The different orders of the priesthood became the Occult Bodies within the Christian Church, and up to the Middle Ages the priests in the Church possessed all the knowledge of Occultism that the world had. And the Catholic Church is now the only one that has preserved a trace of this ancient truth. It was during the Middle Ages that the Occultists as a class withdrew from the Church of Rome and formed secret bodies or societies, such as the Rosicrucians, in various parts of the world.

At the present day almost all occult knowledge is possessed and preserved by secret societies; and the members of these societies or bodies only teach such individuals as have reached a point in their evolution which has made them capable of receiving the higher truths. In this way portions of this secret knowledge are given to the world from time to time as the world becomes able to receive them.

The culmination of what is known as the Dark Age, in this period of evolution, came in the nineteenth century, for at that time the world reached its lowest point in materialism, and from now the tendency will continue to be upward toward Spirituality. A few Occultists believe that the time has passed when there is a necessity for guarding these secrets with such jealous care, and believe that the world is ready to receive more of these truths than formerly. Then, too, many persons are making discoveries along these lines and are ignorantly misusing the forces they are learning to use. So it has been decided to teach the people something about these forces and how they can and should be used, in the hope of averting, if possible, the fate of the Lemurians and Atlanteans.

Almost every day you may see in the newspapers advertisements in which the offer is made to instruct people concerning personal magnetism

and how to use it; how to be successful, how to
become popular and how to dominate other minds
until they become enslaved.   The people are
awakening and are beginning to feel a great desire
to know about these Occult forces; and if they do
not use them rightly they will surely use them
wrongly.

At the present time various efforts are being
made to give the occult teachings to such persons
as are fitted to receive them, but they cannot yet
be taught in full to the great mass of people;
but should only be given to those who desire to
know the truth and who wish to ally their forces
with those of Nature for the good of others and
for benefit to themselves.

Now you are not going to be taught all there is
about Occultism in these lectures, but only that
particular portion which teaches what the great
Universal Mind is; and after that what you are,
what your subjective and objective minds are and
what occult forces each of these minds reaches
and controls.   Then you shall be taught how to
use these forces for your own upbuilding and for
the hastening of your evolution.   We shall confine ourselves to mental lines, taking fragments
of occult history and bringing them together into
a small mosaic which will show you your relationship to the Universal Mind and how all humanity
is but a manifestation of that great Mind.   We

shall learn how to build ourselves up along spiritual, mental and material lines, because this knowledge can be used successfully along all three. We all want to succeed in life materially, and most of us want to grow in knowledge and power; and it is through the use of these forces that we accomplish our heart's desire. The time is fast approaching when man must learn to use his mental forces or fail in the great evolutionary struggle—fail for this entire period—not to take the battle up again until some other Cosmic Day shall come. In the course of time all men who survive will become Occultists.

LECTURE TWO

THE God idea seems to be universal, although we are told that in the interior of Australia a tribe of men was discovered who had no conception of God. In all my investigations that is the only mention I have ever seen of a body of people who were entirely without any idea of God or of what is generally meant by the word God. This idea concerning Deity changes as man develops. It was the late Colonel Ingersoll who had a very clever and profound way of stating this thought. He said, "An honest God is the noblest work of man."

This is profound because man's concept of Deity corresponds with his power of idealization; he cannot create a God that is above his own ideal. And while it is true that God created man in His own image, according to the Scripture, it is also true that undeveloped man is forever returning the compliment by creating God in his own image. Therefore when primitive man began to realize the "I am I," that is to say, that he was something distinct and apart from everything

24

else, he came to the point where he began to manifest the principle of self-consciousness; he began to think, to analyze and to worship. The first thing he saw which awakened a feeling of fear or reverence in him was what we call Nature and natural forces; and perceiving that they were stronger than himself he commenced to worship them as his Deity. Next he passed on to the making of an image of the thing he worshiped, such as the totem; and later he worshiped the sun and moon and stars. When he had learned by experience that fire could destroy both his body and his possessions he began to worship that too, and thus he continued to live for ages alternately worshiping and propitiating everything which he did not understand and could not control.

The idea of Deity is first found in individual worship. Each man has his own particular God which is a true one for him, because each person has his own conception of Deity. But as he becomes stronger he is not satisfied to worship alone and then he desires to impress his ideas upon those with whom he comes in contact and we find him in the second stage of his worship, which is tribal. When a certain tribe of men becomes stronger numerically than another and begins to dominate that other it immediately enforces its own God idea upon the conquered people as was most excellently illustrated in the primitive Grecian States. There every little state had its own particular God, but as the states became merged a national God idea gradually took form, by the weaker states accepting the God of the stronger. But sometimes the tribal or national God of the conquered people appealed to the wants or needs of the conquerors and was adopted by them as when Isis became Diana of Ephesus. Christianity has given us another example of this adoption of another nation's God by accepting Judea's God Jah-hovah and renaming Him Jehovah.

Jah-hovah was nothing more than the Male-female creative principle united. It was a Planetary Spirit or one of the Elohim. Christianity adopted Him from Judaism and improved upon the conception of its votaries by making of Him a Universo-personal God. Much of His supposed wrath and vengeance was modified or ameliorated by attributing to Him enough of the element of love to enable Him to show a leniency toward such of His creatures as He had elected or foreordained to be saved.

But now we have passed into a transition state and man's conception of Deity is broadening from the anthropomorphic to a real Universal God without modifications or limitations. The anthropomorphic idea means God made in the image of man or ascribing human attributes to God. In olden times the attributes of human weaknesses and human traits were ascribed to the Jehovic God. But we have now arrived at the point where anthropomorphism is no longer characteristic of the most progressive thinkers. We are now able to conceive of a Universal Deity; one without human weakness, one without human limitation; and if there is one thing above all others that this great mental and metaphysical movement stands for it is the sweeping away of the old anthropomorphic idea and the giving in its place a Universal Deity.

"Divine Mind" has been selected for the term to be applied to this new conception of God in order to emphasize this idea of Universal Deity; in order to bring out clearly first the Deific idea and secondly the fact that it is consciousness. I prefer the term "Universal Consciousness," but since "Divine Mind" seems to be a favorite term with the Christian Scientists, the Mental Scientists, the "New Thought Movement" and others, we shall use that as representing the universality of Divine Consciousness.

This consciousness being universal necessarily manifests everywhere. Looking at it on the objective side and in the mineral kingdom we speak of the cohesion of minerals. Now minerals cannot be cohesive unless there is a certain amount of consciousness to hold them together. If we examine into what we call the transition states, or if we go back of the mineral kingdom to the gases which chemicalized to produce the minerals, we find something we call chemical affinity, which is a certain form of consciousness. Let us take a concrete example. A drop of water is, as you know, formed by the combination of two gases, hydrogen and oxygen in parts of two to one, H_2O. Why should they unite in this combination rather than in any other? The amount of power required to disrupt the forces locked up in that drop of water is something tremendous. Yet you may take a drop of water and put it on a piece of iron and you can watch the divorce as it takes place between the two elements. If there were no consciousness in what is called chemical affinity this could not occur. The tremendous force locked into that combination of gases becomes dissipated as soon as the atoms are brought into new conditions. This shows that there is consciousness there; were it otherwise no change would have taken place. In the case of boiling water: if fire and water were but inert matter acting upon inert matter and no consciousness were there, how could those vibrations be raised and the water be made to boil? But it is the conscious side of the atoms composing the fire, acting upon the conscious side of the atoms composing the water, which raises those slower vibrations of the water and makes it boil.

Passing up a step higher we come to examine the vegetable kingdom. Why do pine, hemlock and spruce trees grow side by side taking from the earth only such particles as each needs to sustain its individual life? Is there not here a conscious selection of elements made by each tree?

In the animal kingdom this consciousness becomes so distinctly individualized that to distinguish its higher form from the lower or vegetable kingdom we call it something more than consciousness—we call it intelligence. In man we find a still higher form of consciousness than in that of the animal, which we designate as Mind; and this state of development is the highest with which we are familiar. Therefore when we use the term Universal Consciousness or Divine Mind, we mean that which comprehends, that which embodies and includes all that we call consciousness, individualized or otherwise. We mean all that is visible or invisible, known or unknown. All that can be seen, touched, handled or sensed; all that can be apprehended—all is God.

The Universal Mind consists of two portions—the manifested and the unmanifested. The manifested portion can be apprehended by the human mind, but that which is unmanifested cannot be apprehended. There is a plus element which is always above and beyond that which is manifested. The manifestation takes place within the unmanifested and there is always something from within which brings forth the manifested. The plus element we shall not attempt to explain; because I am informed that none of the Occultists —not even the greatest—has ever been able to fathom all of Its nature.

From man's point of view the manifested portion of the Universal Mind consists of two parts, the visible and the invisible; and yet each of these is but a condition, a part or a diversity of the complete unity of the Universal Consciousness. Divine Mind or Consciousness expresses Itself in the two great forms which are popularly known as force and matter: looking at matter from the standpoint of a materialist (because matter is what we are supposed to be most familiar with) we will study the manifestation of the Universal Consciousness in that form.

We are supposed to be familiar with matter, and yet Holman J. Clerk-Maxwell and almost all scientists are willing to confess that their conception of it is but a hypothetical idea. Huxley, in his "Sensation and Sensiferous Organs," says: "All that we know about matter is that it is the hypothetical substance of physical phenomena." Physically we can know very little of either force or matter because this objective world is on the plane of effects.

The Occultists divide matter into two great portions, the particled and the unparticled. The particled portion comes forth from the unparticled as a precipitation of it. Let me try to make this clear to you. If you place a pan of water outside your window when the temperature of the atmosphere is below freezing point, you will find that gradually there is a lowering of the rate of vibration of the atoms which compose the water until there comes a crystalline formation within the pan. Most of the water in the pan is still fluidic, but there are also these crystalline formations, and we have both the particled and the unparticled portions in the pan. In a like manner throughout Nature these two forms of matter are forever seen during a period of manifestation or evolution, and it is the particled portion of matter that science has agreed to call atoms, though I believe that recently certain scientists are trying to sub-divide even the atom which they admit they have never yet seen. There are several scientific theories concerning the nature of the atom which we will not discuss at this time. It is sufficient to know that the physicists agree in saying that logically and necessarily there must be an ultimate element, and this produces the phenomena which we call physical life.

It has often seemed to me that if all Mental Scientists had the faith of the profane scientists they would soon become Occultists and would ac-

complish anything they undertook, for the profane
scientist—if the term "profane" will be excused
—says: "Such a law must of necessity exist,"
and often stakes his life upon his faith. Then,
too, he always lives up to and acts upon his scientific faith. For instance, before Neptune was discovered science said: "At such a point in space
there should be a planet," and thenceforth all
astronomical calculations were based upon this
logical theory; but it was not until a long time
after the scientists had made known their theory
that the planet was actually discovered. And so
it is with this question that we are considering
—the existence of the unseen atom. The scientist
knows that there is a unit of substance; he knows
there must be one because visible physical forms
are the product of something and he says they
must have an individual basis and therefore there
is an atom.

The Occultist asserts that the atom which the
scientist says must exist, does exist, and is visible
upon the subjective side of life. It is the smallest
portion of particled substance, and atoms are the
bricks with which the world is builded. So the
atom is seen and known by the Occultist and is
recognized as a logical necessity by the physicist.
Then comes the question, how is it created?

The Occultist says it is created by the will of
Deity. Deity desires to manifest, to raise Itself

to a higher form of existence, and this desire going forth within Itself causes the Universe to grow into objectivity. This desire manifests first in the particled portion and is a force which being sent into unparticled matter causes a precipitate within itself which is called atoms. And all worlds, all bodies, all atoms are made of the same substance. Everywhere throughout space there is but one basis for the physical universe and this basis we agree to call matter. Most people, however, give to matter qualities that it does not possess and therefore give it a power over themselves. If you understand the nature of matter and look at it from the right standpoint you will be able to control it; but if you give to it qualities that do not belong to it then it will control or limit you.

The other great power which is recognized as a factor in building the physical world is force, and we find a limited amount of knowledge concerning it. True it is that scientists have classified forces as electric force, force of heat, force of steam, etc., but after everything has been stated and analyzed we find all that the physicist knows of force is that it is the immediate cause of a change in the velocity or direction of the motion of a body. In other words, it is the proximate cause of the phenomena of form. When we view the material world as the manifestation

of Deity we know that behind this motion which
we call force, and behind this form which we call
matter there is a cause which produces them;
and we want to know something about this
cause.

The Occultist starts with the premise, as we
said before, that all is Deity or Divine Essence.
This Divine Essence manifesting as motion is
called force by both the Occultist and the physicist. The Occultist also calls it thought because
all force in its ultimate is either thought or the
result of thought. With the Occultist force and
thought are identical and force is the product of
mind. The Divine Essence manifesting as matter is what both the physicists and Occultists call
substance—substance being the collective name
for the atoms; and we call it substance because
it is that which stands under, that which lies behind the visible Universe. The physical Universe
is, therefore, but atoms in motion or vibration
and back of matter and back of motion is Divine
Essence.

The mistake that the physicists of the ultra
school make is in believing that matter is all;
that everything is a by-product of matter and
that Mind and Consciousness are but this thing
which we call matter in motion. And the great
mistake of the ultra Mental and Christian Scientists is in believing that all is mind and that there

is no matter. Each view is extreme, and fails to distinguish both manifestations of Divine Essence. The Divine Essence does manifest in those two forms and we should study its manifestations in both; therefore, to say there is no matter and thus sweep away in thought the physical world is, in my opinion, not altogether scientific. But the true scientific attitude is to say that the Supreme Universal Divine Essence—Consciousness—God—does manifest in the dual way of motion and matter. This gives us the trinity of Consciousness, Force and Substance.

The Occultist does not forget this trinity and the part each portion plays in life. The atom as viewed by the Occultist is dual, and has its consciousness or force aspect and its substance aspect. Its positive aspect is consciousness, its negative aspect is substance, and these two are inseparable.

The physicist does not recognize the force side of the atom as consciousness and the Christian Scientist does not recognize the physical side, but the Occultist maintains that the physical side of the atom is the vehicle for consciousness; and this duality of the atom is the keynote to Occultism. The knowledge of this is essential to the conscious production of phenomena. Understanding this, you may realize how the visible Universe is produced, how forces are controlled, how cures are performed by mental therapeutics. It all resolves itself into the action of mind upon mind or upon lesser and other forms of consciousness. Matter is subject to mind when mind controls form through the consciousness side of substance, by making and modifying vibrations, the cause of form.

The world of form is but atoms vibrating at certain established rates. Vibrations which appeal to us as sound have no inherent sound, but are due to rates of vibration that impinge upon the nerves of the ear and are transmitted as vibrations to the brain and thence to the mind. Those vibrations which appeal to the eye as color have no light per se, but are rates of vibration that impinge upon the optic nerves and are transmitted to the brain as vibrations. All is vibration— vibration modified by Consciousness behind it or by individual consciousness within it. All sensation is but the effect of vibration upon the mind.

For example: I am looking at a glass bulb that contains an electric light. It gives me the impression of something we call light. The ether is made to vibrate at a certain rate and these vibrations impinge upon the optic nerves and reach the objective mind within the brain, and I have the sensation of something we have agreed to call light. Thus we see that it all comes back to a mental basis for a material world; since all kinds of physical phenomena are produced by the same substance vibrating at different rates.

For example, hold a poker in the fire. After a while it becomes so brilliant that we call it white. Then take it out of the fire and watch it. After a little time it will change from white to yellow, then to red, and finally back to black. It was the same group of atoms vibrating at different rates which produced the separate and distinct colors of the poker. The impinging of the vibrations upon our minds caused our conceptions of the changing colors; and the same law which produced the colors for us produces the physical Universe or the external manifested world. Therefore it is the relationship of our individual consciousness to the external world of vibrations which makes the world for us.

Now let us consider Divine Mind in its subjective manifestations. The lower portion of the particled part of that Consciousness is, in the scientific phraseology of the physicist, the ether. The two are identical. Ether, like the atom, is something that the scientific world says must exist; it is a logical necessity, but no scientist has ever seen the ether; he only knows that it produces or in it are produced certain phenomena. This ether is a subtle, universal, magnetic, fluidic medium in which all manifested things are embedded: this is about the consensus of the opinion of the scientific world.

We will now consider these qualities of the ether from a mental viewpoint, because this course is particularly designed to teach you the nature and powers of mind.

First of all the ether is subtle. It interpenetrates all other forms of existence, all other forms of physical life. Why do you see me? Why do you see the light? Because of this subtle essence that is between us. I am talking about an aspect of the Universal Mind and you must remember that this subtle essence is Consciousness. You are permeated with it, the atoms of your body are held together in groups by it; this subtle consciousness is in every portion of your being. You are swimming, living, existing in a sea of it.

Secondly, we must understand that the ether is universal; it cannot be excluded from any plane or place. This Universal Consciousness is, as its name implies, everywhere. It is important to remember this universality because in thought transference or in treating mentally a person at a distance you must realize that there is no separateness in consciousness. Upon the plane of mind the thought passes immediately from one to another; so you do not have to make a great effort to reach another mind. You can reach it instantly and easily through the medium of this consciousness because it is universal.

Thirdly, the ether is magnetic. It attracts all its parts, and every part and particle of itself being interdependent none is independent. Every particled part of this sea of magnetism, every individualized part, whether it be an atom, a man or a sun, is a magnetic center; and because the whole is magnetic each part must be magnetic. Evolution can only be carried on by reason of these centers and it was for this purpose that they were brought into existence. Every center in the Universal Consciousness should be preserved. Therefore your first duty to God and to yourself is to preserve your own magnetic center. Occultism teaches no sacrifice of self, because evolution would be retarded instead of aided by such teaching.

By this I do not wish to be misunderstood as saying there should be no self-denial, or that there should be no giving up of personal or selfish comforts or superfluities; but I do mean that the individual center should not be destroyed or depleted until it becomes an imperfect medium for Deity to work through. Occultism says no one should sacrifice his life for another because every life is important to Deity, and for aught we know the life to be sacrificed may be the more important center of the two at that juncture of history.

I am not speaking of sentimentality, but I am stating a law.

Again, no one should give and continue to give of his own spiritual, mental or physical force until he is a bankrupt. A depleted center is of no use to Deity in the evolutionary struggle. Look over the list of those persons who are practicing mental therapeutics, or think of your altruistic friends who are bearing other people's burdens and see how the law has acted in their cases. Are not many of them mentally, physically or financially depleted and of comparatively little utility because of this conscious or unconscious violation of the law? I am not eulogizing heroics, sounding the glory of martyrdom nor criticizing the victims of vanity; but I am stating an immutable law.

I know that altruism is said to have been taught by the Nazarene Occultist, and admitting that after three or four generations had passed away, He was correctly reported in this respect—in the records which you now have—then His teachings could only have been intended to neutralize the intense and almost universal selfishness which prevailed at that time. Both altruism and selfishness are extreme views, while intelligent individualism is the middle ground and is in accordance with the law that I have stated. It is fortunate, however, that selfishness is so earnestly condemned and that altruism is more preached than practiced, or humanity would not be able to press on in compliance with the law as it is doing at present. So your duty to yourself and to Deity is to become a positive center; and the higher your rate of vibration the more powerful do you become. No one ever succeeded in life who was continually in a negative condition. To be successful you must be positive. "Unstable as water, thou shalt not excel," says the Scripture. You must be strong and positive, and then whatever you undertake will end successfully.

Did you ever stand on the bank of a river and watch the water as it whirled round a center or vortex in the stream? Did you observe how that vortex drew to itself everything that came floating down upon the current? That was an active, positive center distinct from any other center or vortex in that stream, and because of its individualized strength it had the power of attraction and everything was drawn into it.

So it is that men become vortices in this great magnetic sea of consciousness and according as they become positive and strong do they draw to themselves whatsoever they desire. But we cannot help others until we become strong ourselves. We must have force before we can impart it to others. We must know before we can teach.

Fourth, the ether is fluidic. This particled sea of Divine Consciousness flows according to the impetus given to it both by Deity Itself and by man; and it moves in the direction in which it is sent. This is another important fact to remember because you will learn that there are currents within this fluidic sea and later on you will be taught how to attach yourself to those currents and forces and to draw such as you desire into yourself. There are also currents of love and you shall be taught how to attach yourself to draw love to you. There are destructive currents and you shall be taught how to avoid attaching yourself to them.

Suppose you were a thousand miles from home and you desired to help some member of your family. With your power of thought you could make this fluidic force, this Consciousness and life flow into the person that you desire to help. So it is very important that you should realize something about the nature of this fluidic Universal Consciousness. It is a wonderful storehouse in which everything that is conceivable to the mind of man is stored; and his thoughts going forth into it can bring back to him just what he desires.

Fifth, this Consciousness—the ether—is the medium in which all things are embedded and through which all things are connected with each other. Because it is a medium there is no friction between any parts of it per se; it yields to you and yet connects you with any or all of its parts.

It does not impair or retard the force you sent out into it, and it brings back to you precisely what you send forth. If you think love to a friend, your love will go to him precisely as you think it, and with no greater nor less intensity than you feel it. If there were any friction in this Universal Ether or Divine Consciousness we should not be able to receive the light from the stars. The worlds would some time stop in their orbits because no world would be able to revolve for more than a limited time, if there were the least resistance to its progress through space.

Consciously direct your thought into the Ether and it is sure to reach the person, place or thing to which you send it. If you want to give me a mental treatment, you think kindly, positively of me, and this thought going from you into the Ether makes a little pathway for itself until it reaches me. For the time being there is a magnetic cord established between us and over that magnetic cord you send your thoughts of health and strength. No wave of thought vibration can ever be impaired. Modern scientists agree that at the same place and at the same time there may be an infinite variety of etheric waves of different lengths, with none of them interfering with each other. We can see waves, which we call light, as they are sent to us from the stars; and could we but translate the messages those waves of light or vibrations are bringing to us, we should be wiser and better than we are. But Occultists know that the color of a star indicates its state of development, and in this way we are able to determine which of the heavenly bodies are below or above us in their evolution.

Most persons know scarcely anything about the magnetic power which is daily given to all living creatures by our sun. We know that the sunshine often dispels the fears which have come upon us at night. We know that difficulties which seem insurmountable as viewed by moonlight, melt before us like mist when the beautiful, golden rays of the sun are turned upon them. We may be courageous, positive and strong while the sun shines, but when it has disappeared below the horizon and the shadows of night have settled down upon us our courage dwindles, and we often become weak and negative. More souls pass out of their bodies at night than while the sun is shining; and people who are ill grow worse as the sun commences to decline. All these conditions are governed by the law of vibration. The light waves or vibrations from the sun are the strongest, the most powerful and the most magnetic that come to us from any source. They are a continuous flow of force currents to this world and to all other planets near enough to receive their vibrations. When a person or any

other individualized consciousness concentrates
its thoughts upon the sun it receives a mental and
a magnetic treatment from that great center,
since the concentration of thought opens a direct
channel for the great force to flow through to the
one concentrating upon it; and the vibrations both
mental and physical of that person or creature
are raised in proportion to the intensity of its
powers of concentration.

Divine Mind is precisely analogous to a sensitive plate and each human thought makes a picture on that plate. By thought you make the
exposure, and the thing pictured will in time become your own, for you are attached to your
creations and time develops the picture for you.
If you hold the image you have made long enough
you will get a perfect picture; if you think idly,
then you have made what the photographers
would call an under exposure and the picture is
not full, clear and perfect, and many of the details
are left out; but by holding the picture firmly
and strongly, you make it a permanency and then
it is yours, for thoughts become things.

Mental pictures are first mental things, but
after a time they become physical things or draw
physical things to them, for the great Consciousness gives back to us precisely what we send into
it. It gives to us whatever we ask of it, and our
ignorance in making demands will be no protec-

tion to us. The only way that evolution can go on is by Divine Mind granting every request that we persistently make; it is in this way we gain wisdom through experience.

This automatic action, as it were, of Divine Consciousness was fully taught by Jesus, but is as little understood or believed in by His present so-called followers as it was by those whom He originally tried to teach. You remember He said: "Judge not that ye be not judged; for with what judgment ye judge ye shall be judged; and with what measure ye mete it shall be measured to you again." And again He said: "Ask, and it shall be given unto you; seek, and ye shall find; knock, and it shall be opened unto you." And when He said these things He was stating what He knew was a law which could be put into operation then or at any time afterwards.

LECTURE THREE

IF we let a ray of light pass through a series of colored glasses we find that the color of the last glass it passes through is the tint that the light will take; and the tint of the light will be accentuated because the colored glass modifies certain other colors not consonant with its own nature, while it permits the rays of a similar vibration to its own to pass through. The same conditions hold good with consciousness. Consciousness is limited in its manifestation by the medium or media through which it manifests. For an illustration, take the consciousness of a flower, an animal, and a man. There is a limitation of the expression in each of these, by reason of the form in which it manifests. And consciousness also accentuates the peculiar nature through which it manifests. It accentuates that particular portion of the Universe, or planet, or man, in which it manifests.

Concentrate your consciousness—your mind—on your right foot, and hold it there for a while, and you will draw the blood from other parts of

47

the body into the foot, until it will become swollen and red. You are thinking of the foot to the exclusion of all the rest of the body. That portion of your consciousness which is functioning in the foot is accentuated above the consciousness which remains in the rest of the body. Carry this a step further, and we find that the law operates precisely in the same manner with the entire man. Consciousness accentuates that portion of the man in which its greatest expression is. For that reason, since the early Christian centuries the body has been mistaken for the man, because it was the last medium through which his consciousness or mind expressed itself—it was that portion of the man which was accentuated by the consciousness.

Very little was known of the real nature of man after the second and third centuries of the Christian era, except that he was a body which was generally regarded as the man. The theologians knew there was a body, and, consequently, in their theology the body was put forth primarily as man. They thought he had a soul, and taught certain doctrines concerning that indefinite something which they designated as his soul. This term "soul" is still somewhat indefinite at the present day. Any of the leading dictionaries will give you a large variety of meanings attached to the word. The theologians could not define or picture the soul, but they accepted the Jewish conception of the Adamic man, and believed that Adam was created out of the dust of the ground; and that afterward God breathed into him the breath of life; and they regarded that breath as his soul.

We find in the Hebrew Scriptures—the Old Testament—the expression, a "nephesh for a nephesh" (a life for a life), and "He that taketh the nephesh of his neighbor's ox," etc., showing that the exoteric Jews had no conception of a soul as distinct from the Universal life principle— and they have very little conception of it to-day. So when the Christians rendered in theological language the Jewish thought, they called the life principle of man his soul. Later in the centuries the "moral philosophers" appeared on the scene, and were almost as indefinite in their teachings concerning his true nature as were the theologians. These moral philosophers—whom we now call metaphysicians—also taught something about a soul or mind; but there was a confusion of words, due, of course, to a confusion of thought, and instead of teaching what soul or mind was, they described the phenomena of mind.

For instance, in the writings of Sir William Hamilton, who was one of the representative thinkers of his time, which was not far from our own age, we read the discussions concerning mind, and we find the question: how many articles or subjects can the human mind be conscious of at one time? Also discussions of the peculiar phases of sleep-walking, unconscious memory, etc.; in other words, the study of the *phenomena of mind.* All the Occidental ancient moral philosophy concerning the inner mind, soul or spirit, as they were indefinitely designated, was really what we now call physiological psychology, and pertained entirely to the action of mind upon or through the body.

Since the consciousness manifested chiefly in the external man in those days, and since the body, plus a little indefinite something more, was regarded as the man, it was only natural that the theologians should have taught the doctrine of a physical resurrection. Many of them did not know how to account for immortality unless there was to be a physical resurrection—at least this was true after the Council of Nice. We find at that time that the Christian and the Jew were the only two religionists in the world who feared a dissolution of the physical body; and naturally there arose the barbaric practice of burying dead bodies for the purpose of preserving them. The Egyptians preserved their dead only for the supposed purpose of having their old atoms to use again on their return to earth.

The majority of people of the present day have

not progressed much further than the theologians
and the metaphysicians of the early centuries.
Ask ten men whom you may meet in every-day
life, what a man is, and nine of them will describe
the physical body. You will be surprised to learn
how little is known of anything besides the
physiological man. I have been told by persons
who were considered intelligent, that the soul is
a body something like the physical, only more
beautiful, because it has wings like a bird; and I
believe that was the common conception of the
people of the middle ages. Many of the old paint-
ings represent the soul as a body, floating through
space with a pair of wings. The body, plus wings,
was the artistic conception of the psychic or real
man in ancient Christian times.

A few days ago I asked a well known Church
woman in the city, what she thought a soul looked
like. After considerable thought upon the subject
she replied that she did not know, but supposed
it was something white that fluttered like a sheet
in the wind. I asked another the same question,
and she said she was not certain, but thought it
was something like an alarm clock attached to
the body, which kept ringing when one did something one ought not to do. With nine-tenths of
the people there is no distinction between themselves and their bodies, for man knows very little
of himself at the present time; and it would be

well for each of you to stop now and see what definition you can formulate concerning yourself.

In the middle of the nineteenth century, the more adventurous minds commenced to investigate the nature of man and the fact of whether or not immortality was demonstrable, and there arose what is known as the Spiritualistic movement, or Spiritualism. In this country, and in France, the investigators maintain that there is a persistency of consciousness after the dissolution of the physical body, and that certain phenomena are produced by it. This was the first general deliberate attempt in Christian times to discover the soul of man, and the first effort to collect a sufficient amount of scientific data on which to base a philosophy concerning the psychic man. They have given us no philosophy yet, although their investigations commenced sometime in the middle of the last century. The principal tenet of their belief is that beyond this earth life there is somewhere an eternal progression for the human soul, which certainly is an improvement on the old orthodox Christian belief in stagnation by reason of the wearing of crowns, waving of palms, and singing hallelujahs forever and forever.

The next movement along this line commenced in 1875, and was known as the Theosophical movement. This was started for the purpose of studying, among other things, man, and particularly his latent psychic faculties. This movement gave a more exhaustive and complete theory concerning the nature of man than was then to be had in the Occident. Vague it was at times, and the several sections of the movement differed in belief among themselves. Some made man a combination of seven, and others of fourteen, different personalities or principles; but, nevertheless, it was an attempt to reach something besides the physical.

In 1886 there was another movement along the line of investigation of psychic phenomena. This was called the Society for Psychical Research, and worked along the same general lines that the Spiritualists were investigating. The object to be attained was to establish *scientific* demonstrations of the persistency of man's consciousness after death, and many scholarly men and women became investigators with this object in view. If anything more than what the Spiritualists had learned before them has been gained along this line it has not been reported to the world, though I have no doubt that any real genuine enlightenment from this society would be thankfully received by many.

Finally came that body of investigators whose practice is called Hypnotism, and which is mesmerism, revamped and renamed. Hypnotism has done a little good for the world, and it will do

considerable harm before it becomes generally
condemned. We want to see the good in everything, so I shall call your attention to a few facts
that Hypnotism has brought forth. It has proved
to the minds of many, and it has certainly given
evidence to the minds of all who have investigated
it, that the body of man is not the man. For when
a person is put into the state of hypnosis, the body
is unable to think, to feel, or to function in any
way. If the body were the man, sleep could not
extinguish entirely his consciousness; there would
be enough left to register sensation. If you stick
a pin into the flesh of a man in ordinary sleep you
will get a quick response, and unless you are very
active you may regret making the investigation.
But if you stick a pin into the flesh of a man
who is in a state of complete hypnosis, you will
find there is no response from your victim. This
shows that in one case there is consciousness, and
in the other there is none. This evidence is sufficient to prove to the unprejudiced investigator
that the body is not the man, but there is within
the body a recording something that is capable of
sensing things external to the body. The phenomena of Hypnotism also show that the mind is
not the product of the molecular vibration of the
brain, because during hypnosis, and while the
brain is quiescent, the mind continues to be
active.

These experiments are further verified by the use of anæsthetics. When a person is etherized, the effect is the same as if he were hypnotized; because in both cases the mind, or the real man, is forced out of his physical body, which is then incapable of functioning, and remains inert until the reasoning principle returns to its habitation. Many times, a subject has been put into hypnosis and the consciousness sent out of the body to a distant place, whence it has brought a correct report of things that were occurring there at that time. Hypnotism, therefore, has done two very good things. It has scientifically proved that man is mind, the thinker, and that mind can persist separate and apart from its vehicle, the body; and if that condition can exist for one moment, then there is no logical reason why it should not exist throughout eternity. Hence we have here some scientific data for immortality.

Investigations upon these subjects were first made in recent times in Paris, and in Nancy, France; afterward in the United States and in Sweden, and finally throughout the world. Investigators found that there was a mind, capable of experiencing sensations, which ordinarily functioned in the human body but which could be separated from it as I have just described. But they also found that there is a secondary mind in man, and that after the first mind is well under the control of the hypnotist, there is still a secondary mind or intelligence which may act independently of the first. This secondary consciousness they named the subliminal self. So they have found that man is not only a mind, but he is two minds. In the course of time the first consciousness that was reached became known as the objective mind, and the second consciousness as the subjective mind.

If mind is something—and Hypnotism has shown that it is—then mind must have a form and a color. We cannot conceive of anything in the Universe that is without form and color. Individualization, separateness, requires form and color, or those conditions could not exist. A great mass of evidence has been collected from various sources upon this subject. Spiritualistic Societies, the Society for Psychical Research, and clairvoyants, seers and sensitives all over the world agree upon the one point that mind has form. They differ somewhat upon the question of whether or not it has color, but that is a logical necessity. They say that mind has form, and that its form is the same as that of the body which it inhabits, and that the real man is an etherealized prototype of his physical self. In other words, the physical self is but a materialized picture of the inner man or mind. All evidence agrees on that point, and if human testimony is worth anything, it is certainly conclusive in this case, because there is a unanimity of evidence from four great sources which do not harmonize on many other points.

About color there is a great difference of opinion, due to a difference in the respective development of the observers. Let me illustrate. A woman is walking along the street, and observes another woman approaching. She says: "What a beautiful dress," and is asked what is its color, and answers "blue." She is asked how it is made, but can only say that its general effect is beautiful, and its color is blue.

Another woman who saw the dress would tell you its color and how it was made. Still another would agree with both the others, and would add, "And the woman who wore the dress was more beautiful than her dress." The last observer was able to see not only the dress, the design, and the figure, but also the character of the woman within.

It is the same with the four classes of observers or investigators that have been mentioned; some are persons who ordinarily function solely upon the objective plane of life, but who, under exceptional conditions, sometimes see the outlines or figure of the psychic or real man. Other more careful observers having advanced to the point where they can command the higher natural forces, and can function upon the subjective side of life, may see not only the outlines of these mind or soul forms, but see them as plainly as they see physical forms around them in the ordinary affairs of life. Then there are others who have advanced so far in their evolution that they can look beneath the form of the man and see the character. These persons are the Seers, or higher Clairvoyants. The last two classes agree with the Occultist in making the assertion that the character of mind is always known by its color; and this must be scientifically true, because there could be no differentiation of form except through the vibration which manifests as color. So it is a logical necessity, as well as a matter of testimony, that every human mind or psychic man has form and color.

There is one thing in the world that cannot lie, and that thing is vibration. The vibrations of a man determine his form and his color. And his thought or character is the cause of his vibrations, as we shall see later, in another lecture. As far as we have gone we have learned that man is identical with mind, and that this mind has form and color; also that man has two consciousnesses which are called the objective and the subjective minds. The normal color of the subjective mind of man —known in the theological parlance as spirit—is yellow or blue. It is of the same nature as the Ether or Divine Consciousness whence it came.

The color of the objective mind of man—called by the theologians the soul—is green; and man's predominating color is always determined by the mind which dominates. Having arrived at this point, we will now examine the origin of these respective aspects of man, the objective and the subjective.

Evolution is not carried on equally throughout all its parts. We find this is true wherever we investigate the operations of this law. But Evolution is carried on by the creation of centers within the Great Consciousness, and by enlarging and preserving these centers. As actual reform is carried on in a great city by the reformation first of individuals, and not with trying to reform the whole public at once, so it is with the great law which works through centers or individuals.

The Occultist differs from the physicist in his views of the law which governs natural selection. The physicist illustrates the working of this law in a manner something like this: A little Hottentot, who represents the highest degree of development in his particular locality, wanders into the forest, and meets another little Hottentot who is the highest exponent of the development of another tribe. These two, being male and female, meet by chance, and by natural impulse or selection marry, and raise a family of little Hottentots to a higher degree of development than themselves. This is the law of natural selection, and chance determines the entire evolutionary career of the race, according to the physicist.

But the Occultist has a maxim that "nature, unaided, fails," and believes that there could be no evolution except by working through conscious centers. For instance, our sun is a center purposely formed, and through that center great life force is consciously sent out to smaller, weaker centers, imbuing them with life, and promoting other forms of life and growth upon them as it does upon this planet of ours. It is the same with species and types; it is not a natural selection, in the sense of nature working blindly, that causes evolution, but it is rather an artificial selection, or the raising up of individual parts. Take man, for instance; the Adept selects such advanced men and women as he knows are capable of evolving more rapidly than others, and by putting his own force and strength upon them he aids in their development, and in this way these selected individuals are assisted upward till they become the highest expressions of manhood and womanhood.

In the animal and vegetable kingdoms man takes the highest expression of this or that form or type, and through artificial, conscious selection, unites them with other forms, and thus produces a higher type of expression, as in the breeding of animals and the grafting of trees and flowers.

The Occultist insists that the purposiveness of Deity, as Nature, is present in all Its individual parts but becomes fully manifested only through the conscious co-operation of the more evolved centers of Itself.

Understanding this we are now prepared to examine the origin and development of the subjective and objective minds of man. In passing, it should be stated that while we will use the terms objective and subjective mind as being one of the accepted expressions of the modern psychologists, we do not fully endorse their views as to the nature and power of those respective minds.

First, then, as to the origin of the subjective mind. The Occultists teach that the subjective mind of man came direct from the substance of Deity, much as Athene sprang from the head of Zeus. With the co-operation of the Elohim— those great Ones who said "Let us make man in our own image," the Supreme Consciousness coalesced within Itself quantities of Its particled portion until mind forms were created. The atoms were drawn together by the power of attraction, and it was thus that the subjective minds of men were born. Let us illustrate:

Imagine the atmosphere to be the Supreme Consciousness. Look forth into it on a cloudless day. The atmosphere itself is heterogeneous matter and is ordinarily invisible. After a while

you may see a gradual condensation of some portion of the atmosphere, a center is being formed,
a cloud appears which is of the same nature as a
part of the atmosphere, and sufficiently condensed
to become visible to you. It is in this manner
that individual minds are born out of the Ether.
Take again as an illustration something we have
used before—a pan of freezing water. At first
the water is homogeneous; then there is a lowering of the rates of vibration of the atoms that
compose it, and gradually some tiny crystalline
forms appear. These crystalline forms are attracted, and small pieces of ice appear in the pan.
This ice is of the same nature as the water, yet
it is separate and distinct from·it. It is in the
same manner that the substance of Deity is condensed and the individual subjective minds of
men are born. Those of you who have read my
wife's occult novel, "Mata, the Magician," will
remember this same thought is there poetically
and beautifully expressed, as follows:

"It thinks, and Suns spring into shape;
It wills, and Worlds disintegrate;
It loves, and Souls are born."

It is not my purpose to enter into the details
of the working of the law of evolution, but to help
you understand your own nature I shall give

briefly an outline of the evolutionary steps that are taken by the subjective mind in its process of individualization. As you have seen, an immediate condensation of consciousness within the Great Consciousness is caused by the desire of Deity to manifest or express Itself in individualized forms, and this expression is brought into actuality through the instrumentality of the Planetary Spirits, or Elohim. These great Beings send Their thoughts to a designated point in the Ether, form a center, and through the vibrations of Their united thought-forces cause an assembling of atoms whose conscious sides respond to these vibrations.

The physicists tell us that with the grouping of atoms into molecular life a new individuality is always created, which is something more than the sum total of its constituent parts. The Occultist says this is true because the union of the conscious side of the atoms causes the character or individuality to appear in the group. So, when the many atomic consciousnesses are compressed into an oval form by the Elohim, there comes into being an organized consciousness or mind, which controls its atomic parts. These Ether-born minds thenceforth take up their evolution and gather and store their experience as they progress, and by such methods become more and more individualized. The evolution of these subjective minds begins upon the subjective side of life, and for ages they continue to progress upon planets that are composed of such tenuous matter that they are invisible to the present sight of men. After these subjective minds have become thoroughly individualized, they—or rather we, for these subjective minds are ourselves—become ready to incarnate in animal forms on this physical world of ours.

There are two classes of subjective minds which always incarnate at the same time on a physical world. Those who have been created for that planetary chain of graduated worlds, and those who have attempted their evolutionary career before on some other planetary chain, but who failed, and are now making another attempt to go on in their evolution. For a center of consciousness may not be successful in the particular period of evolution in which it is first brought into existence; and salvation is not a mere matter of faith or belief alone. It depends entirely upon one's self whether one reaches Godhood from manhood in the evolutionary period in which one sets out.

Until a certain point in the evolutionary career of man and this planet was reached, the Universal Consciousness pushed men forward. After that point was passed, and men had reached their mental majority, and should have become indi-

vidualized, the old order of things was changed.
Men must use their own minds now, and must
make use of the knowledge they have of Nature's
laws, if they expect to go on in their evolution.
It is progress, or fail and return into space, to
remain until a new period of evolution shall commence on another chain of planets, when souls
shall again attempt to perpetuate their individuality. Ultimately, man's destiny is to evolve
to something higher than manhood—he is to some
time reach Godhood, if he perseveres.

Your attention will now be called to one or two
characteristics of the divine portion of man. The
subjective mind is the divine nature, because it
comes direct from the Great Universal Consciousness; it is the Logos, or the Word made flesh.
It is the highest because it is the first expression
of the Universal Consciousness; it is close to the
heart of God, is the first born, and carries the
first impress of Deity. Because its evolution was
entirely subjective before it reached this planet,
and because it now functions normally on the
plane of causes—the mental plane—it is the intuitive portion of man. It is that portion which
knows without reasoning, which apprehends immediately upon the presentation of a subject; that
which sees causes.

The objective mind evolves entirely upon this
planet. It is an offspring of this particular period

of evolution and of this world, and its nature is the result of its objective growth and physical experiences. Briefly, its evolution is as follows: Deity settles down as a great mass or cloud of consciousness upon a planet, and vitalizes it, and gives to the mineral kingdom its form of consciousness by ensouling it. I do not mean you to understand that this lower kingdom becomes wholly individualized. For instance, in the vast fields of coal and iron the Great Consciousness has not individualized because that form of expression restricts individualization; but when we examine the higher portion of this kingdom—the precious stones—we find that here, in a measure, individualization has begun. A part of the mass, a few of the purest and best atoms, those which are capable of taking a more rapid rate of vibration, have become separated from the others, and have made an attempt at individualization. Then a part of the Great Consciousness passes on to the vegetable kingdom, where we have first the lichens and grasses; each of these is a separate and distinct form, and consciousness is there individualized; but the individualization is not perpetual because of the frailty and lack of persistence of the forms. Thence the consciousness passes into the bush, and afterward it reaches perfect individualization in the tree, the highest form of life in the vegetable world.

Then a portion of the Great Consciousness sweeps on into the animal kingdom and ensouls the lowest animal forms, and gradually, as evolution prepares better vehicles, these souls of animals, or individualized intelligences, re-embody themselves in higher physical forms of animals, until we have the elephant, the horse and the dog. Here individualization becomes not only consciousness, but it becomes mind, and persists as animal mind. It re-embodies itself in one form after another, and the dog, for instance, comes back many times to this material plane a dog, and gains more strength and knowledge by its experiences. Finally these individualized animal minds pass into the ape forms, and thence into physical human bodies, and though these bodies disintegrate and pass away, the animal minds persist and reincarnate and ultimately become the objective minds of men.

When these quasi-human forms have reached the point of development where they are capable of becoming vehicles for the Divine Subjective minds, then the union of the subjective and objective minds takes place. The subjective minds come to earth for the purpose of getting experience upon this material plane, that they may become wiser, and more strongly individualized; also that they may raise the animal minds or objective consciousnesses, which they ensoul, to a higher and a better condition of development; for with the interblending of the Divine Subjective mind with the objective or animal mind comes a permanent union, and those "whom God hath joined together" cannot be separated without a tremendous loss to each, as will be shown in the lecture on "Lesser Occult or Psychic Forces and their Dangers."

After the union of the subjective and objective minds has taken place, this *united* entity continues to incarnate and re-incarnate as its physical bodies wear out. Understanding this, you will be better able to appreciate the meaning of Chapter Six of Genesis, where it says: "And it came to pass, when (animal) men began to multiply on the face of the earth, and daughters were born to them (that is, when sufficient forms were created), that the sons of God (the subjective minds) saw the daughters of men (the objective minds) that they were fair; and they took them wives (blended with them) of all which they chose."

Genesis is the disarranged, mutilated remnant of a Chaldean occult record, and even in its present form, with the interpolations it has received, it contains great truths. Some day an Occultist may re-arrange the original parts of the Bible, and interpret it for the enlightenment of the world, but as it is, it contains much for those who are able to read and understand.

intelligence, is
:y of man; it is
icated through
ooks; it is that
ι; and it is also
ere not for the
l, as was shown
.otism. The ob-
lesignated as the
ins its knowledge
tener wrong than
s. It only takes
na, and then, not
ses it is incapable
lusion.
as incarnated into
real psychic man,
iding of these two
n, and in that form
not physical man
oecause of the form
the model for the
physical body.   _   ian is the magnetic
matrix into which the physical particles are built.
Thus it is that all form has its mental basis.
Before a form can exist on the physical plane it
must be created on the mental plane.

Since both these minds are condensations of
the Universal Mind, they both have naturally the

characteristics of that Mind. The Universal Consciousness brought them into existence through Its creative capacity, so both these minds have the power of creating. The great trouble, however, is this: the objective mind, through its animal experience, has acquired the animal fear. This is the chief characteristic of the animal mind and is its mainspring of action; hence most of the creations of the objective mind are the product of fear or are colored by fear.

For example, our mothers stamp fear upon us before we are born, and continue to do it after we are born, and until we have grown old enough to fear for ourselves. They create diseases for us through their fears of disease until we get old enough to create our own diseases. And that wretched fear follows us from the cradle to the grave. We are afraid we shall not succeed in business, and we create our own failures. We fear we shall not have money enough to pay our bills for the current month, and we generally lack something because we have created that lack. We fear bad luck, disasters, and death, and it is indeed a wonder that man has not swept himself off this planet through his fearful creations. The offspring of fear are the creatures and creations of this objective mind; and the subjective mind which is within the objective mind accepts the unfortunate creations, believes the misrepresenta-

tions, and unites its own forces with those of the
objective mind in bringing the pictured calamities
into real external existence.

For example, I once knew a little girl who was
named after her aunt, and her mother often said
to the child: ''I hope you will not have a cancer,
and die with it, as your aunt did.'' After a time
a small bunch appeared on the child's cheek—
following an abrasure—and her mother said:
''That looks as if it might become a cancer.''
After a while, when the child's attention was called
to the tiny bunch on her face, she would gravely
declare that it was her cancer. Her mother
had suggested the thought, and the little one
had accepted it. When she grew to womanhood the cancer developed, as the mother and
child had feared it would, and it had to be
removed.

I knew a man who was very fortunate in business and was successful in everything he undertook. One day a friend said to him: ''Your luck
can't always go one way.'' Very soon he began
to think about that remark, and after a while he
accepted it as a prophecy, and then began looking
for his good luck to change to bad. Soon little
things began to go wrong, and every time some
misfortune came to him he remembered what his
friend had said. Then he commenced looking for
mishaps everywhere, and within five years from

the time he accepted the unfortunate suggestion he was ruined financially and physically.

Here are three rules which it might be well for you to remember in this connection:

First. The dominant consciousness always controls the creations.

Second. The environment shows which consciousness controls.

Third. Ignorance of the laws of life excuses no one.

If you continue to create ignorantly you will suffer the same as though you knew the law, because an unwise use of the law brings unfortunate results the same as the wise use of the law brings good results. God always gives you in time precisely what you create, and if you allow your objective mind to do the creating you must accept its creations; your ignorance will not excuse you. If you should kill a man because you were angry, whether you knew it was against the law of the State, or not, you would be punished. It is the same with the moral law. Both your minds can create good, but the objective mind usually does not do so until it has been properly trained. The subjective mind of man must control the objective mind and its fears before he can make pictures that will bring him pleasant environment. Every time an unpleasant thought or fear comes to your mind, banish it. Every time a thought of disease comes, blot it out. You can do it, because you have the divine power, and can control your objective mind which is your instrument and vehicle. If a mental picture of disease comes into your mind and you let it remain, it will become a physical reality; but if you destroy it the moment you see it, nothing can come from it. In the place of a picture that you do not like, make one that you do like. Make your thought picture, and God, in time, will fulfill your desires thus expressed. But you never will be successful, you never will reach the highest of your possibilities until you control your own objective mind and its forces. How to do that we will take up in the next lecture, which we will call "The Art of Self-Control."

One more word in regard to the dual man, which is mind. This dual nature of mind or man will explain many of the contradictions of human nature. It will give a full explanation of original sin, which is nothing more nor less than the uncontrolled animal nature of the objective mind, which expresses itself whenever and wherever the opportunity is given, until it has been disciplined. If you want a colt to become a racehorse you will take great care to have it thoroughly broken and trained before you enter it for a race; and still you permit the animal objective mind of your own nature to remain untrained, and to dominate you while you are trying to use it in the race of life.

If you remember the distinction of this dual nature of mind you will understand what has paralyzed the force of the Christian Scientists and has filled them with great terror. They describe a something outside of Deity that is not divine, but which creates, but can only create evil. They do not know where it comes from; they merely know it is in man. That cult calls it malicious animal magnetism, and makes of it a personal devil; but it is nothing but the objective mind of man, uncontrolled. It is a part of the Universal Consciousness, and therefore not devoid of good. It is more ignorant than bad, and makes mistaken creations in its undeveloped state.

Understanding the lower nature of man, you understand the nature of evil. Evil is but the creations through ignorance of this objective mind. It is a misdirection of the creative forces; it is the permitting of the unenlightened animal mind to make creations. Many of the old theological questions and the Christian and Mental Science questions of modern times are understood, and are explainable, when one understands the dual mind of man.

LECTURE FOUR

ONE of the reputed wisest men that ever lived said: "He that is slow to anger is better than the mighty; and he that ruleth his spirit than he that taketh a city." Of course I refer to Solomon.

This lecture on "The Art of Self-Control" might be said to be an amplification of that utterance of Solomon. I am free to admit that it is much easier to talk about self-control than it is to practice it, but, nevertheless, there are certain ways whereby we can, in a measure, exercise self-control. The fact that Solomon made the remark quoted does not appeal to one particularly, unless one can see the reason for so acting. There are persons who, if they read *in the Scriptures* that certain things should be done, will do them because the Scriptures command them to be done. And there are persons who will do things because their parents or someone whom they love or honor says such a thing should be done. In such cases the effort is but a perfunctory one, unless a reason for so acting be given, and very little good comes of the obedience to the command

75

under either of those circumstances. Let us see
if there is a reason for Solomon's aphorism.

It goes without saying that no one can be truly
great who has not the power of self-control. It
does not matter how many virtues a man may
have, if he allows himself to give way to
paroxysms of anger and loses his self-control at
critical moments, his greatness becomes largely
diminished; neither can he become really successful in any chosen field or line of work unless he
has first developed self-control. Napoleon said
if he could keep his anger below his chin he could
control men. In other words, when his emotions
became dominant then self-control was lost and
when he lost control of himself he had no power
to control others. Grant's great strength lay in
his power of self-control at critical moments.
George Dewey destroyed the Spanish Fleet
quickly and completely because he controlled himself first and afterward his men. His command
to his Captain was: "When you are ready,
Gridley, you may fire." Imagine, if you can, a
statesman who has not developed this art of self-
control and you will find that at the moment he
needs self-mastery most it utterly deserts him.
Imagine one of the great financiers of this country
not having sufficient control over his tongue to
keep his plans secret, and how long would he be
a factor in the world of finance?

In the case of physical health, unless there is an approximate control of the emotions, there will never be permanent good health, because there cannot be perfect health without perfect self-control. The reactions which naturally follow outbursts of emotions bring about physical disorder; if not immediately, then in the course of time. And above all, there can be no progress made in Occultism unless there be self-control; and that which really determines the growth of a student is his power to control himself. Without this power, intuition cannot be fully awakened, clairvoyance and clairaudience cannot manifest and his development is otherwise greatly retarded. A student cannot make use of the higher forces of nature unless he becomes self-controlled first. A mental healer cannot assist or relieve a patient so long as he is in a perturbed condition of mind himself. A student cannot dominate his own body unless his mind is poised and undisturbed. He cannot concentrate on a person at a distance and get his thoughts, unless he has the power to make his own objective mind quiescent while the power of concentration is put into action.

Some of the reasons I have given why we should master the art of self-control may not interest or appeal to many of you from an intellectual standpoint, but here is one that may. Every time you lose your self-control, your aura or photosphere becomes so actively inharmonious that all the creations you wish to draw to you are repelled. You cannot be a successful creator upon the spiritual, mental or physical planes unless you are able to control your emotions sufficiently to enable that which you have created to come to you. Another reason for exercising self-control is this: One can never escape from pain until self-control is acquired. One can never reach the place of peace until the conquest of self is made.

As understood by the Occultist, self-control is the control of the objective mind by the subjective mind. Another way of expressing the same thing is to say that self-control is the control of the emotions by the higher mind. This latter statement may seem more tangible to you. Sensations and emotions are the manifestations of the objective mind of man as we have heretofore seen.

One complete conquest of the objective mind by the subjective mind is sufficient to establish self-mastery. In other words, we do not have a new objective mind to conquer in each natural incarnation. To illustrate this let us take hydrogen to represent the objective mind and oxygen to represent the subjective mind. Now the time for the union of the two minds has come and the oxygen blends with the hydrogen making a drop of water. The union of the two in the drop of water corresponds to the union which makes the real inner man. This drop of water may be at one time in a clay jar, at another time in an iron vessel, and another day in a crockery bowl, and then in a Dresden cup; it is the same drop of water no matter what its environment may be. And so it is during all your different incarnations; there is but one entity, the psychic man, who is composed of these two minds incarnating together in different physical bodies; and if you once conquer your objective mind you will be its ruler throughout eternity. Looked at in this light, it does not seem such a hard thing to do when you consider that you have only one conquest to make. But while there may be but one conquest there will be many battles to fight and it is during these battles that victory is constantly shifting, sometimes being on on side and sometimes on the other; but finally the conquest must be made by the subjective mind.

In the early part of our evolution the pleasures of physical and animal life seem to be greater than the pain and consequently the subjective mind, in order that it might receive the pleasures of sensation, permits the objective mind to have absolute dominion. But any force grows with use and the objective mind, as it manifests itself more and more, becomes so strong that finally the reactions that follow pleasure bring more pain than pleasure, and the subjective mind awakens to the situation and begins to demand a way out of pain. We have been indulging in these sensual pleasures during all the ages past; life after life we have given way to the objective mind, and have allowed it absolute sway and dominion, because we thought there was more pleasure to be had out of life in that way. But reactions came and pain taught us that there is a better way to live. Pain is the evidence that the objective mind has not been fully conquered.

In the last lecture you were shown some of the characteristics of both minds, but there are a few other facts which I will mention which may possibly help you to identify yourselves with the subjective mind, or your real self. The subjective mind is the "I am I" of man; it is the self-consciousness, or that part of him which studies the states of his consciousness and modes of mind. It is the center of consciousness in him and until it has been awakened there can be no self-control. Emotions will not control themselves, and, as the term implies, there must be a Self which can control them. There are two aspects of both these minds, the positive and the negative. In the subjective mind the negative side is the intellectual and the positive side is the will. But at this period in our history the intellectual side of our natures is awakened and the will is not. The

objective mind also has two aspects, the negative
or reasoning side, and the positive side or desire.
These two aspects in the objective mind are
blended to a large extent and because they are
thus united that mind is strong.

Our first great object should be to awaken the
will portion or force aspect of the subjective
mind, in order that the will and the intellect,
united, may control the objective mind. There is
force enough in the positive side of this subjective
mind to accomplish anything it desires and therefore it is to our interest to awaken this latent but
tremendous force in ourselves. Let us see how
it works. I say I wish to do something. That is
the desire or the positive side of my objective
mind expressing itself. But another aspect of my
mind replies: "No, you must not do that because
it is not right." Here are certain aspects of my
two minds in activity, the desire or positive portion of my objective mind and the intellectual or
negative portion of my subjective mind; and if
my will or positive portion of my subjective mind
is not awakened, it will be more than likely that
the positive side of my objective mind will win
the battle. But if the positive side of my objective
mind says I want to do something, and my will
or the positive side of my subjective says: "You
do not want to do anything of the kind and you
shall not," then there is put into action a greater

force than desire and the desire is overcome by
the higher or positive side of my subjective mind
—the will.

The emotions are natural forces on their proper
plane; and because they are natural many persons
think it unnecessary to control them; and many
who would like to control them do not know how
because they do not understand their own natures.
Because a thing is natural is no reason why it
should not be controlled. Electricity is a natural
force. Used properly for illuminating purposes,
it is a very good thing. But it is a natural force
and can be used to destroy human bodies and
valuable property also, so there may be a perversion of natural forces through the misuse of
them, or by not controlling them. To understand
our emotions we must analyze them, since they
seem to make up the greater portion of ourselves,
and their name is legion. In appearance they are
many, and yet, on close analysis, we find only four
basic ones and the battle will not seem so hard
if we can realize this.

The first great emotion, the one that causes us
the most needless suffering, is Fear. The second
cardinal emotion is Sensuousness. The third
basic emotion is Sex Desire; and the fourth, and
most subtle of all, is Vanity. These are the basic
elements of the emotional nature. You cannot
conceive of any emotion that has not its origin

in one or more of these four. Let us briefly examine the nature of each of these emotions, since the larger part of the actions of mankind are directly attributable to one or more of them.

Fear is the cause of most anger, most jealousy, most murder, failure, theft, doubt, discouragement, despondency and many other lesser inharmonious conditions. Analyze any one of these states of mind, and you will find that fear is the father of it. Eliminate fear and you have destroyed the root or basis for many of the emotions which lead men astray. Begin your fight directly upon fear—not the many phases of it— and a tremendous amount of force will be saved; for it must be conquered before very much will be accomplished in life. You remember you were taught in another lecture that the mind is magnetic, and draws to itself whatever it frequently thinks about. When you are constantly fearing something, you are drawing toward you the thing you fear, and the reason humanity has not been swept from this planet long ago is because it has shifted its fears from one object to another so often that it has never held to one thing long enough to destroy itself.

To accomplish rapidly the destruction of this great enemy it is well to begin by controlling some of its grosser forms, such as physical cowardice. Great numbers of men and women are inwardly the most wretched cowards and yet suppress the external expression of their fears because ashamed of them. Here is where the fear of public opinion is greater than the fear of something else, and the emotion is not conquered but shifted. Try to conquer your cowardice, because it is an enemy to you and is retarding your development.

Then there are very few persons who do not fear someone. You may not be conscious of the fact, but if you stop to think, you will see that it is true. You dread to meet Mr. Blank because you do not know what he will think of you, or because he is wealthy and you are not, and you are afraid you cannot make so great a display as he can. Or perhaps you have heard that Mr. Blank is a great statesman, and you are in awe of statesmen; so you stammer and grow red and wish you were a thousand miles away when you are introduced to him. The first thing to do toward overcoming this fear of persons is to declare, "I am not afraid of Mr. Blank, nor of anyone else." Then calling to mind the image of Mr. Blank, say to it as if he were there in person, "Mr. Blank, you have not the power to make me uncomfortable, and I am not afraid of you," and continue to repeat this assertion till your perturbation has subsided and you feel that you could face him without a tremor of fear or embarrassment.

Many women are afraid of mice. I have seen a room full of women put to the most ignominious flight, screaming like lunatics because a tiny mouse ran across the floor. To cowards of that class I would suggest that you put a mouse into a cage and keep it where you can look at it. Examine its little body through a magnifying glass and make friends with it, declaring constantly while you are looking at it that you are not afraid of mice; that there is nothing about them for you to fear; that they are small centers in consciousness and you are a larger center in the same consciousness; that the same life principle that sustains them sustains you; and after you have come to a realizing sense of your relative positions your fears will fade away, never to return.

When you have eliminated the grosser forms of fear, then attack the finer forms, such as fear of the unseen or the unknown. Many persons' lives are made utterly wretched because of their fear of the future. They are continually expecting things that never happen. Others are afraid of the criticism of the world, and a common question on their lips is: "What will people think?" You should remember that the world always criticises and condemns everything and everybody that it does not understand. You must declare, therefore, that you are not afraid of the criticism of any individual nor of the public at large; that you are not dependent upon anyone for your health, wealth or happiness; and that the approval and disapproval of other persons, whether collective or individual, are alike to you. If you declare this earnestly and often you will overcome all fear of criticism.

Fear being eliminated, we next turn our attention to Sensuousness, which is the result of a perversion of natural forces. The animal indulges his senses in order that he may live; but man indulges his senses not only that he may live, but also to get pleasure from his indulgences; and it is the over-indulgence that constitutes the perversion of this natural force. Reaction seldom follows the natural indulgence of the senses for the purpose of living. If a creature eats because he is hungry and stops when the hunger is appeased, there will be no reaction; but when the senses are indulged more for pleasure than from necessity, and there has been an over-stimulation, a reaction always follows the indulgence. Asceticism is one of the moral reactions from sensuousness. In many places in the Orient, especially in India, asceticism is taught as the proper method of living. Many schools of philosophy in America have adopted this Eastern teaching. This is the other extreme, and, like most extreme views, is not productive of the best results; hence the

Western school of Occultists does not agree with the Eastern school on this point, which, after all, is but a question of the method of development. Suppression of the senses is not the best plan, and Western Occultists have found that better results are gained from regulation of the senses. By regulation is meant a moderate indulgence in all that pertains to the normal use of the senses; but never yield to over-indulgence. In this manner you may have all the pleasures of life without the reactions. Sackcloth and ashes do not indicate that the wearer of them has become spiritual. To deny the body its natural functions, or to whip or torture it, does not make a person wise nor good; and there is no more reason in trying to gain spirituality through asceticism than there is through over-indulgence. Use your senses properly and enjoy all the harmless things of life, and let the will—not the desire—determine the extent of the use of the senses. This is regulation, the teaching of Western Occultism.

The third great basic emotion that mankind has to learn to control is sex desire. This, too, is a natural force, and is a part of the force of life and love; it is a part of the force of magnetic attraction, manifested in the Absolute, and manifesting in every part of It according to the nature of its vehicle. In the minerals it is chemical affinity; in the animals it manifests as the desire

for procreation. In man this force, like sensuousness, should be regulated. Here again Western
Occultism differs from the Eastern schools, where
asceticism is taught. In man this emotion should
be so well regulated that it should become a creative force instead of an animal desire for procreation. I do not mean that this force should only
be transmuted into mental power, but that it
should be used to consciously create bodies, un-
marred by passion, for the use of egos who desire
to reincarnate. Use this natural force, but do
not abuse it; regulate it, but do not eradicate it.
The normal condition of man requires that no
part of his body should become atrophied or useless, but that every part of him, whether spiritual,
mental, or physical, shall be in a perfect condition.

The fourth great emotion that must be conquered before perfect self-control is acquired, is
vanity. This emotion is so subtle that at times it
almost baffles us. The peculiarity of this fault is
that the victim does not recognize his defect of
character. You can seldom convince a vain person that he is vain; and because of its subtlety, it
is the hardest and the very last emotion we have
to conquer. The first aspect of this fault is the
grosser or physical vanity which pertains to ad-
miration for its own particular attractiveness of
feature, form or face. It is the feeling which
prompts you to wear a particular style of dress,

not because the dress is beautiful, and because
you love the beautiful, but because you believe
others will admire you in it. It is the same feeling which would cause a person to mutilate his
horse's tail in order to attract the attention of the
public to his horse and then to himself as the
owner of the horse. This grosser form of vanity
we can conquer if we wish to, because occasionally
it is revealed to us by our friends or enemies, and
when it is discovered it can be eradicated. But
this is only the beginning of the battle, because
next beyond and still more subtle, is another phase
of vanity which is mental, and this is still harder
to recognize in ourselves.

Mental vanity expresses itself in all mental
forms. If a man discovers that he is in a small
degree superior to his fellow men he feels it and
often looks with contempt upon his weaker
brothers. He tries to dominate those whom he
believes are his inferiors in intellect, forgetting
the fact that he himself is but a Cosmic infant as
compared with the souls who have passed in evolution beyond him. And it sometimes requires
many incarnations and many sad experiences to
eradicate this defect of character, which really
limits his evolution.

Then comes spiritual vanity, and this is the
force which actuates all reformers. It is this
vanity which makes men say: "All is wrong with

the world.'' It is another way of saying the Supreme Consciousness is wrong in Its management of terrestrial things and *I* must go forth into the world and right it. God has made mistakes, and *I* shall correct them. *I* shall lift all humanity up to *my* plane and help all mankind to *my* level. *I* will convert the world to *my* views, and the people shall accept *my* conception of God, *my* politics, or *my* religion, and men shall be proselyted to *my* truth. Spiritual vanity comes in such a subtle guise that one does not recognize the motive that lies behind one's efforts; and yet the time comes in the evolution of that particular individual when his spiritual vanity must pass away, as it usually does, in martyrdom. There comes a time in that soul's career when this spiritual vanity is burned out of his nature, and he becomes a perfected, self-conscious center in the Universal Consciousness, impersonally working for the raising up of the whole of mankind *according to the Divine plan.* Here is the true At-One-Ment, where your saviours pass away from the adulation and worship of men and become the unseen and generally unknown workers for humanity—the Silent Brotherhood who teach, inspire, and raise humanity as fast as it can receive, with never a word of praise, never a word of recognition, never a word of thanks or of appreciation from the world for their sacrifices and their efforts. Spiritual Vanity must pass away before perfection is reached.

At present we may battle with the first two forms of vanity and leave this last aspect to be conquered in some other incarnation.

Thus we have these four great basic emotions which must be controlled. To do this we must learn to exercise our wills. There are two very good rules by which, if persistently followed, self-control can be attained. The first is, never speak until you have thought with your subjective mind. It will be impossible for you to speak before you have thought at all, because you cannot have a material manifestation of speech until there has been some mental action. But do not let the emotions of the objective mind become expressed in words before you have thought with the subjective mind. In other words, let your thought be divorced from emotion before you attempt to express your thoughts in speech. For example: You walk out of a warm room, suddenly the cold air strikes you, and immediately you exclaim, "I am catching cold!" This remark is the offspring of the emotion fear and is not the result of your becoming conscious of a little fresh air. The objective mind commences to manifest fear and it speaks into existence a creation of sickness. Now if you will stop and think with your subjective mind before you exclaim into existence that cold, and claim it for your own, you will destroy the fear which would be the father of it, and no cold could be created for you.

The second rule is, never act until after you have thought with your subjective mind. Acting upon emotion usually leads to regret and is always followed by a reaction. A thousand cases could be cited to prove the truth of this statement and I have no doubt that you have thought of many examples. These two rules, if put into practice even occasionally, will help you; but if you practice them constantly you will be surprised to see how soon you will begin to dominate the four cardinal emotions; and after they are destroyed, all the others must disappear, because they are but branches from these four principal emotions.

There are certain aids which will assist you to carry out these rules. First, you should realize that all uncontrolled emotions are the result of ignorance or undevelopment; and this knowledge will rob them of their power over you. You will know that you are at the emotional point in your evolution, which is an indication of ignorance of your own power of self-control. Then you will soon begin to see the need of development and set about correcting the fault.

A child fears the dark because he does not know its nature or its cause. If he is carried into a dark room, and the light is turned on, when he sees nothing there to injure him, his fear is immediately dissipated. His fear was banished when his ignorance was destroyed. If you can show a person that there is no "bad luck" except that which he has created, and that the "evil" he fears he builds for himself, immediately you destroy the power he has given to these conceptions. If a man is vain of his knowledge and he can be made to see that the field of knowledge is unlimited, and that his vanity over the small amount that he possesses is but an indication of his great ignorance, immediately his vanity disappears. So it is by enlightenment that any or all of our emotions are controlled or eliminated from us.

The second great aid is this: If we understand what habit is and know the law which underlies it, and if we know that much of our yielding to our lower natures and our lack of self-control is a matter of habit, we shall be able to destroy habits much sooner than if we do not understand them. I cannot enter very fully into this subject at this time, but will give you a good working basis to begin with. There are two elements that enter into the formation of a habit. The first is what we may call the law of periodicity, or periodical return, and the second is the initial impulse. The law of periodicity causes a thought or an act to be repeated within a determinate time. The intensity with which the thought was projected, or the act performed, determines the time in which the tendency to repeat itself will manifest.

Let me try to make this plain to you.   Look at an electric light for a moment, then shut your eyes and note the effects.   Immediately there is a mental vibration or picture of a bright light that passes away after a short time; now it re-appears, to pass away again.   Again it appears and disappears, growing dimmer with each ap-pearance, until finally it fades out altogether. This is an example of the action of the law of periodicity, and every thought, every feeling and every tendency will repeat itself at given periods of time according to the intensity of the initial impulse that gave it birth.   Recognizing this law, if you will remember the exact time your habits repeat themselves, you will be prepared to over-come them with greater success.   What is called the association of ideas is another illustration of the working of the law of periodicity.   For example, if we go to our room, or to any place where we can be alone, and send out an intense thought at nine o'clock in the morning, or at any special hour, we will find on the following day at the same hour that we will be inclined to repeat the thought.   If we yield to our inclination each day, at the end of a week the habit will be formed and it will require some effort to resist the temptation to repeat the practice we have begun. This is the way habits are formed through the cyclic law bringing back to us the thoughts and things we ourselves have created. Someone may say to me, "You are going to lose something," and my heart will almost stop beating as the picture is presented to my mind. The next time I see the person who made the suggestion of loss that same picture will rise up in my mind because I associate that person with the suggestion made to me. When I pass the place where we were when the suggestion was made I will remember it and tremble with fear, and after a while the habit of thought will become so firmly established with me that I will think of the loss predicted until the picture materializes, and becomes a reality on the objective plane.

But the same law which helped you form the habit will help you overcome it if you but reverse the rule in this way: When the mental picture recurs, destroy it by denying that it can materialize. For example: If you have been holding a picture of loss, declare that you cannot lose anything that belongs to you; and when your picture of loss comes up, refuse to look at it and put into its place a picture of something that you want. If you have a habit of thinking of yourself as an invalid, destroy that habit of thought by picturing yourself in the possession of perfect health. If you have created the habit of picturing death for yourself, or for a friend, reverse the picture and see him and yourself well and happy; and the law of periodicity will bring your new pictures along with the old ones, since they are associated together. Each time both pictures appear, look at the new and refuse to see the old and soon the old picture will fade out and disappear and a new order of things will be established.

The third great aid in conquering the emotions is through the power of suggestion. Heretofore the objective mind has been making most of the suggestions which the subjective mind has passively received. For example: You feel a draft of cold air, and immediately your objective mind suggests to your subjective mind, which is really you, that you are taking cold; you accept the suggestion, and reply, "Yes, that is true; I shall take cold if I sit in this draft;" and immediately you commence to see the picture of yourself with a cold. You have accepted the suggestion and claimed the creation of the objective mind for your own, and there is nothing that will prevent the picture from materializing for you. But if you will use the same amount of force in refusing to accept the suggestion of your objective mind that you do fighting the cold after it has materialized you will not let it materialize at all.

If you desire to conquer the emotion sensuousness, and your objective mind insists upon gratifying its appetite for the pleasure of eating, you should take the position that you do not want any more food and should suggest to your objective mind that *it* does not want any more. Speak to it as if it were another person or a child. If you have the habit of drinking, or smoking, and you wish to overcome these habits, suggest to your objective mind that it does not want to drink or smoke; that there is no real pleasure to be derived from the gratification of these tastes or appetites, and you will soon see, if you persist in this use of suggestion, that your desires will change, and you will conquer sensuousness without a great deal of inconvenience or annoyance.

There are certain declarations and suggestions that most persons who work along this line find extremely beneficial and I will give you a few of them. Suggest to your objective mind: "I am your master, and you are my servant, my instrument, and you must obey me." If you persist in making this declaration you will soon begin to feel that you are master, and your objective mind must accept it as the truth; and as soon as both minds recognize the truth of that declaration from that moment self-control is assured.

Another way to take from the objective mind its power over the subjective mind is to declare

"You cannot control me," or "You cannot disturb or make me uncomfortable." The word *"cannot"* expresses limitation always; used in the proper place, it destroys wrong creations; used improperly, it limits one's power to progress. It is useless to argue with the objective mind, because it is a waste of force; one might as well argue with an animal and expect to convince it of the error of its ways. The only way to be successful in conquering it is to command and compel it to obey, and when it attempts to argue with you command it to be silent. Say "Peace, be still," and let that be your answer to all its protests and arguments; and the greater the vehemence with which you speak these words, the sooner will the objective mind obey you.

Separate yourself from your objective mind in thought, and for convenience while learning to master it, identify it with your body. Realize that you are separate from, and superior to, it; treat it as if it were a child entrusted to your care by Deity to educate and enlighten. While you are putting into practice these suggestions, demand daily from the Supreme Power the highest wisdom that you are capable of receiving, and "all things whatsoever ye shall ask in prayer, believing, ye shall receive."

LECTURE FIVE

THE LAW OF RE-EMBODIMENT

HERBERT SPENCER, in his "First Principles," discusses force and matter, and after a long dissertation he accepts as a fact the indestructibility of matter and the persistency of force. The idea he develops is that it makes no difference how often matter and force may change form, nevertheless they are persistent; therefore he argues that there is only a certain amount of force and matter in the Universe. He concludes his discussion with the opinion that in his judgment the whole Universe is an unfoldment from the homogeneous to the heterogeneous and back to the homogeneous again; and these respective periods he designates as "alternate eras of evolution and dissolution."

In his statement that the whole Universe is a manifestation of alternate eras of evolution and dissolution, Mr. Spencer has touched upon an Occult truth, a fragment of Occult knowledge. For the Occultist teaches that there is no such thing as eternity, as understood by the Western mind; that nothing can go on working forever and forever without rest. His idea being that everything moves according to given law, within certain periods, and that there are actions and reactions throughout all nature. Those of you who are familiar with the Eastern philosophy, will remember that this same thought is brought out there, and is described as "the days and nights of Brahmâ." Occultism says that the Great Consciousness manifests Itself periodically as the Universe, and after each manifestation there comes a period of rest, a period of night; for even Divine Consciousness Itself must rest.

When the Night of Brahmâ is coming on, gradually the living Universe finds its life pulsations growing slower and slower, and fainter and fainter; and one by one the planets fade from sight; one by one the stars cease to give forth their light, and the suns themselves grow dim. The Earth is rolled up as a parchment, and men and gods and worlds and suns all sink into sleep —there are no thoughts in the Great Mind. All is silence, rest, darkness. Reaction has followed action; the day's work has been done throughout all parts of the Supreme, and the Cosmic Night has come.

This night of rest lasts Eons embracing thousands and untold thousands of years; then comes creation's dawn. There is a slight pulsation within the Great Consciousness and there begin to be the rudiments of the Universe. It is as though one were standing in a great dark auditorium in the center of which burns a flickering flame of light. It is the only point of light to be seen in all that great place; then away in the distance another flame appears, then another and another, till the heavy atmosphere begins to pulsate and soon every portion of the room is illuminated, and that which was darkness becomes light, and the non-existent exists and becomes motion. You who have stood upon an eminence and watched a city as darkness was settling upon it saw, as the night advanced, one tiny point of light after another appear, now here, now there, until there was a great blaze of light throughout the whole city, and where it had been obscuration and gloom it became a brilliant illumination.

So it is with the Great Consciousness. From Its innermost heart goes forth the pulsating life, and the Solar Deities, in whom are embodied the greatest power and wisdom that man can conceive, are awakened to take up their part of the work in the new day, and there a sun springs into existence, then another, and another, until the whole Universe is again brought into activity. These Deities radiate the life force which thrills into activity the Planetary Spirits, who also take up their work, and worlds come forth into space again. These Spirits radiate the life force that awakens the lesser Gods who have slept through the long night of Brahmâ, and they resume again their evolutionary journey. And so the morning of a Cosmic Day has come. Deity has awakened, and has planned the day.

The Cosmic Days are more or less alike, as are all the days of men's years alike, except that each Cosmic Day is better than the one preceding it, since each new period of evolution is an advance beyond the one that passed before. Divine Mind images within Itself, or pictures the new day, and thus creates the outline of the plan by which all things shall evolve during that period. Then the greatest centers of consciousness take the plan as imaged by Deity and carry into execution the idea of the Great Architect. God thinks and the creative agencies bring into existence the physical worlds according to God's idea which they see. God wills and divides into two parts which we have described in a previous lecture as the particled and the unparticled portions, and there is the force and matter ensouled by consciousness. Then by Their will power the great centers of consciousness direct this force and this matter into the different matrices that Deity has planned, and the suns are formed to give forth light, and the worlds are made for men and animals to evolve upon.

The plans made by Deity in the dawn of each

Cosmic Day are what men call "Natural Laws."
They are the ways in which Deity selects to manifest during that particular Cosmic Day. These
plans emanating from the center of the Supreme
radiate throughout every part and portion of It;
and the law which governs the visible side of life
is the same law that governs the invisible side;
and if you find a law operating in the realm of
physics, you may know that it also operates in the
realm of metaphysics.

And now we have seen how Divine Thought
has manifested Itself in physical re-embodiment
and how the law of periodicity has once again
caused thought to be embodied in form, and how
thereafter the law of periodicity makes itself felt
everywhere throughout the Cosmic Day. Take,
for example, the greatest conception of time that
the human mind is capable of actually grasping,
the cyclic motion of our sun. We find that it
travels from a given point in space through its
orbit, and returns again in about twenty-five thousand and nine hundred years. The law of periodicity has caused that great orb to go forth and
return and a cycle has been made. The moon
also has its particular orbit as has our earth and
all the planets that swing in space; all are governed by the law of periodicity. Then again there
is history repeating itself, and man forming his
habits by a repetition of thought. And as it is

with the law of periodicity, so it is with all the other impulses which are sent into the Universe by Deity; they continue to manifest over and over again from the moment they are sent forth until the last throb of the great Deific heart shall be given and the Cosmic Night shall come. The impulses which form a Universe, persist throughout the Universe, and manifest as the Laws of the Universe.

When we find that the Supreme Consciousness re-embodies Itself for a new Cosmic Day we know that the law of re-embodiment must apply to every part and portion of the Universe; that re-embodiment is a Cosmic Law, a law of nature. For evidence of this truth let us study the planets. Worlds are brought into existence by Planetary Spirits or Elohim who see the Divine thought or picture of worlds and use the images for matrices. They then project their thoughts into these centers, thereby creating vortices, which, through the intensity of their vibrations and the tremendous velocity with which they revolve, draw from boundless space the tiny particles we call atoms, and these seething masses of matter become huge balls of flaming gases. After ages and ages have passed these burning balls cool sufficiently to sustain vegetable and animal life upon their surfaces. And worlds, like the bodies of men, have their birth, their childhood, maturity and finally

death and disintegration. When death comes to
a world the life principle commences to flow out
of it through various channels into space. It is
seeking new centers in which to re-embody itself;
and with the passing of the life force from a
world we find disintegration taking place. The
atoms which composed the compact mass of the
external world become demagnetized and fall
away from each other, and finally drift away into
space to be attracted by other newer and stronger
magnetic centers, where they become re-embodied
in other worlds in which consciousness may
manifest.

Re-embodiment is a fact in nature, whether you
look at it from an Occult standpoint, or from
that of Herbert Spencer, with his indestructibility
of matter and force re-embodying themselves for
the purpose of evolution. This law of re-embodiment manifests in all planes, upon all worlds or
planets. That we may comprehend it better, let
us look at the action of this law in the several
kingdoms on this world of ours. Starting with
the mineral kingdom, we find there the lowest
expression of embodied consciousness on this
planet, and as typical of that kingdom we will consider the action of this law in coal. Take some
of this coal and burn it. What is the result?
The hard black mass becomes changed into ash
and gas. The ash returns to the earth whence it

came and again forms earth; and the gas which was liberated by the burning comes into contact with the atmosphere under its new condition and becomes separated into its four component parts which we call oxygen, hydrogen, nitrogen and carbon. The oxygen and hydrogen unite and descend again to earth as water. The nitrogen and carbon unite and form the tissues of a plant and again you find the original elements united, with consciousness embodied in the new form, which is now a plant.

Passing on to the vegetable kingdom we see here the same law manifesting, but in a more pronounced manner; for as consciousness becomes more individualized more of God's plans must be manifested through it. As Winter approaches, the life force, which is the animating principle of vegetation, passes down into the roots. The leaves fall to the ground and the consciousness which manifested throughout the plant withdraws itself from the external to the internal and lies dormant and resting, waiting for the impulse which comes with Spring to awaken and arouse it again into action—to bring it into the external —that man's heart may be gladdened by the beauty of its expression. As the life force rises slowly from root to branch in the bush or tree, we see the law at work bringing forth new forms of life in the shape of leaf and bud and we know that re-embodiment is taking place among the shrubs and grasses and trees.

In the bulb family this same law works. The life force sinks into the tiny bulb at the beginning of Autumn and there it lies in silence and in darkness, within that tiny sphere, till the soft breath of Spring warms and raises its vibrations and arouses within its center a desire to again express itself, to appear once more in a newer and a more beautiful form than that of the bulb. And so it begins to re-clothe itself; it draws from earth and air such chemicals as it needs to give material expression to its beautiful soul or self, and behold "the lilies of the field, how they grow, they toil not, neither do they spin, yet I say unto you that even Solomon in all his glory was not arrayed like one of these," in its re-embodiment.

Passing on to the animal kingdom we find the tadpole and caterpillar. Both of these little creatures are good examples of the working of this law. They are individual consciousnesses; and before your eyes the tadpole gradually changes its form until it has a distinctly different body from the one it had at first. Yet the new frog body that can leap and swim and croak is animated by the same consciousness that animated the wriggling little form of the tadpole. The caterpillar, having a limited and loathsome form, desires a fuller and a better expression of itself and passes into a stupor or sleep. Then slowly its old atoms give place to new, which build a better form, until at last the same consciousness which crawled and crept upon the earth has re-clothed or re-embodied itself and with wings of a golden hue it soars from earth to air. And the re-embodiment of the butterfly from the caterpillar is not only an illustration of the working of the law of re-embodiment, but it is typical of the evolution of the soul or mind of man which rises from the lowest depths of ignorance or so-called sin, to manhood and to Godhood.

This same law is operative in the higher forms of animal life and in the life of man; for a law that is a law of nature must persist throughout the Universe. The fact that we do not see the operation of a law is no proof that the law has ceased to act. Nor is the fact that this law manifests differently in different kingdoms and forms, evidence of the limitation or non-existence of the law. Every law manifests in each class of forms alike, but differs in its manifestation in different classes of forms because the consciousness within the form restricts but does not prevent the manifestation. For example, the law of gravity manifests the same in all iron, but manifests differently in different kingdoms and substances.

Individualized consciousness not only re-embodies itself constantly during earth life, but it

re-embodies itself after it drops its entire body.
In other words, it reincarnates. During the
space of every seven years, according to some
schools of medicine, man undergoes a complete
change of body. Is he not therefore in the process
of re-embodying himself by this constant renewal
of his atoms? According to his rates of vibration
or as his thoughts are elevated or debased does
he draw new atoms into himself. And after he
has dropped one physical body that he has drawn
to himself is it surprising that he should have the
power to draw to himself another? Is the fact
that most men do not remember their past lives
a proof that they did not formerly exist? If so,
the majority of men did not exist during the
first three years of their present lives nor in
a pre-natal condition. The Occultists say that
man does remember his past lives when his subjective mind controls his objective mind—and can
function through it—for in the subjective are
stored the memories of past experiences. What
we call ''Conscience'' is but this memory of past
experiences warning us not to repeat former fol-
lies and mistakes.

Since we have spoken of the re-embodiment of
man by the term popularly known as reincarna-
tion, it may be well before we take up other
aspects of it to answer a question which is now
in the minds of a number of you, and that is:

what becomes of man between the times of his embodiments or incarnations?

As there are different states of matter in this objective physical world of ours, such as gases, liquids and solids, so there are different states of matter in the subjective world; and these different grades do not lie separate and distinct from each other. For example, on the physical plane there are conditions where substances interblend, as it were, as they do in a syphon bottle of aerated water, or in a water-soaked sponge, where each substance occupies the same space while lying within the other. Again, we have the solid earth with certain waters within and on the earth. Outside the earth we have water or vapor in clouds and yet within both the earth and the clouds is air or gases which extend still further out into space.

On the subjective side of life there are finer forms of matter which interpenetrate our earth, water and gas. Around our earth there are belts or zones composed of finer matter very much like the rings around Saturn, and the densest of these rings interpenetrates our earth, while each of the other rings extends further and further into space —according to its rarity and size. These rings are material, but each is of a different tenuity of matter caused by its different rates of vibration. We might crudely picture our world as a porous wooden ball floating in a tub of water. The water would correspond to the first subjective plane and would not only surround the ball, but it would be through the ball as well. Outside the water and surrounding it would be a belt of atmosphere representing the second subjective plane and outside of that would be a belt of ether representing the third subjective plane.

It is to these several belts that man goes between his incarnations; and it is to the first belt, that one which interpenetrates the earth, that the souls or minds of the animals go. According to a man's rate of vibration or specific gravity is he drawn into one or another of those inner belts or spheres which corresponds to, or is harmonious with, his own vibrations. The subjective belts or spheres are not, as many think, for the growth and development of man, but are places of rest where he reviews the experiences and assimilates the knowledge gained on earth. For it is impossible for man to pass beyond the photosphere of this earth and incarnate upon other planets—as some modern metaphysicians claim he does—until his vibrations, which control his specific gravity, have become so high, so God-like, that the law of gravity operating here can no longer confine him to the earth or to the subjective planes surrounding it.

A man's thoughts are the cause of his vibrations, hence a man who is material, sensuous and sensual, is by harmonious vibration drawn to the first subjective plane and becomes earthbound. He cannot rise higher than any other animal, and so he remains in the first belt which surrounds and interpenetrates the material world until he is ready to reincarnate. But as a man's mentality overcomes his emotions, in his course of evolution, and as his subjective mind learns to control his objective mind, he becomes more spiritual; his rates of vibration become higher, and then when the time comes to rest between incarnations he is drawn to the belt which is of a higher rate of vibration, and goes further away from this earth. So, according to the theologians, there is a Heaven and according to Occultism there are several Heavens.

And now comes a very important point in the mental aspect of this law of re-embodiment, which is the practical side of it. Man is not only a center of consciousness, but he is a center of self-consciousness. He has free will within certain great latitudes, and he has freedom of choice, and that fact holds him to a great responsibility. Man, by his choice, or thinking, determines not only his Heaven, but also his earth life. He directs both the time of his incarnation or re-embodiment and the environment of his re-embodiment. The less developed an ego, the more rest does it require between earth lives. This is a general truth and applies to every living thing. For example, you would not expect a child to work as hard or as continuously as a man; you would not expect so much of an undeveloped man along any line as you would of a developed man: and so it is that the thought or development of a man determines the length of time which must elapse between re-embodiments for him. Weak, tired, disappointed souls, they who are ignorant of the laws of life, require a long time between incarnations. It is said by those who know, that the average period between incarnations at this time in our evolution is five hundred years for the great mass of men who are not developed. According to the strength of an ego and its desire to evolve, and therefore its desire to have a vehicle through which to evolve, does the period of time between incarnations lessen or lengthen; and I am informed that among progressive egos the time between incarnations averages now about one hundred years. You can readily see that the shorter the time between re-embodiments, the more experience must be gained; and the more knowledge carried over from one embodiment to another, the more rapid is our progress on our evolutionary journey. Occultists believe it to be advantageous for a soul to keep his body for a very long time; or, in other words, to prolong each of his incarnations to as great a length as it is possible to do. It is a great mistake to cast aside a body before it has become so old and worn that it is no longer of any use as a vehicle.

Every moment of our lives we are changing our bodies and are making them better or worse by our thoughts. We are also creating our environment, liberating or enslaving ourselves, according to the quality of our thoughts and emotions. We create ties between ourselves and other souls through hating as much as through loving because whatever our minds dwell upon, that we draw to us. For example: If I think of you, immediately there is a vibration in the ether between you and me. If I continue to think of you, this vibration becomes intensified until a blue magnetic cord becomes established between us—a mental telegraph wire, if you choose—over which my thoughts pass to you, and by which yours come to me. This connection is visible to the clairvoyant, but not to the physical eye, and can only be destroyed by disuse for a greater or shorter lapse of time according to its size and strength. As a spider spins his web from one point to another, so do men constantly spin thought webs connecting themselves for good or ill with persons or things. If you hate a person, you are continually sending hateful thoughts to that person and by so doing you keep a constant vibration of the ether between you. After a time this vibration becomes a real pathway for your thoughts to travel upon and it binds you to the object of your hatred with a bond invisible yet stronger, and harder to break, than a bond of steel. This is the reason groups of egos come back to earth and incarnate in families and communities. Those who love each other are drawn again and again into the closer relationships of life, not because "blood is thicker than water," but because of the ties formed in past lives.

Then there is the great law of equilibrium, the law of Justice that we are constantly putting into action by our thoughts. This law modifies our evolution, and limits our scope of free will under certain conditions. There is a law of absolute justice and it is man's unjust thoughts which lead him to believe otherwise. Perfect love is synonymous with absolute justice and God is love. If equilibrium were not maintained on all planes, then chaos would reign supreme; it could not be otherwise. On the physical plane we see the manifestation of equilibrium if we look for it. For example, throw a stone into a pool of water, and watch how the disturbance caused by displacing the water at a certain point is adjusted by the movement on the surface of the water from that point to the extreme edge of the pool, and back again to the point of disturbance below the surface. We saw the tiny waves that were created by throwing the stone into the water, but we did not understand that it was the great law of equilibrium working to adjust the water of the pool to the new condition we had created in it. It is through equilibrium that the great law of justice brings back to man precisely what he has sent forth, and this is why he often finds in his every-day life that he must re-adjust himself. "Be not deceived; God (the law) is not mocked; for whatsoever a man soweth that shall he also reap."

In the city of Chicago there is a unique court, called the Infants' Court. It is the only court of the kind in the world and is where infants or minors are tried. Sometimes there are fifty cases tried there in one day, and never less than one hundred in each week. There are cases where parents have abandoned children, or where children have left their parents. Investigation is made into the character and condition of all the children who are brought under its jurisdiction, and an effort is made to place them in the particular walk of life where they may become the best citizens. To a careless observer it would seem that when the Infants' Court had disposed of the child deserted by its parents that would end the matter, but it does not. The Divine Law of Equilibrium caused the child to incarnate through those parents because of associations in a past life. Those parents owed to that child the care and attention it should receive until it should reach an age when it could care for itself; and in order that a perfect equilibrium should be established between those three individuals this child was brought to them to receive that which belonged to it by right. Perhaps the parents did not wish to pay their debt to the child and abandoned it, thinking they were rid of the responsibility, but they were mistaken. Equilibrium; justice, must and will prevail, and if it be not established in this life then it must be in another. That invisible cord created by their thinking in a past life has not been broken by this attempt to shift their paternal responsibilities. Again it will bring these three souls or minds together, perhaps in the relationship of master and slaves, or of mistress and maids, ''For verily I say unto you, till heaven and earth pass, one jot or one tittle shall in no wise pass from the law till all be fulfilled.''

The same law holds good in the betrayal of trust, whether of affections, or of a fiduciary nature. If a person wrongs another, the thought of the wronged one goes forth to that other and binds the two souls or minds together with a bond that cannot be broken until full justice has been done between them.

The general character of a man's thoughts determines his general environment, such as the class into which he will be born; and his special thoughts determine the family in that class which will give him his body. For example, here is a man who cultivates only that which pertains to the so-called evil side of life; this is the side of life that he prefers. He will reincarnate into an environment suitable to the character he has made for himself. He will be born into criminal circles. There is no use wasting tears about him or his depravity; God *is* just, and this universe *is* governed by law. When a man comes back into slum life he has put himself into that condition; his own thoughts have carried him just where he belongs. It is quite common for a soul or mind to incarnate in a respectable circle of society in one life, yet by dissipation, neglect of opportunities, and cultivating the animal side of its nature, to become a social outcast in its next earth life where it will be able to indulge its unfortunate propensities unrestrained by respectable friends or relations.

If a person is born and reared under favorable circumstances, it is because the character of his thoughts brought him into that environment. He was attached by the Great Law to the parents who were able and willing to give him the advantages he received. We could save ourselves much misdirected or wasted force and sympathy if we would recognize the fact that nothing ever happens in this world, but that everything is governed by law. I do not say leave unfortunate souls where you find them, but I say do not attempt to quarrel with the law which is giving to them precisely what they have desired some time in their career. If you see a soul who wants help, then help it; but do not weep over those who are enjoying the fruits of their own thought labors, and do not be dissatisfied, or criticise God because some souls have placed themselves in certain unpleasant walks of life, or have brought upon themselves unhappy conditions.

Man not only determines his birth and the quality of his body at birth, but he modifies his body every moment of his life. Take the dissipated, sensuous and sensual criminal, thinking only of that which pertains to the external side of life; he excarnates, and after a time is brought back to earth into an environment where he is pre-natally marked with the very characteristics that his own mind indicates. He takes that kind of a body which is the best expression for him. It is quite unusual for such a soul to succeed in getting out of that environment in one life, because its body and brain express so strongly those particular characteristics. It is possible, however, for it to do one of two things; indulge in the vicious propensities till the depths of degradation have been reached, and it learns that the price is entirely too great to pay for such pleasures and decides to reform; or it may commence to fight for self-control from the beginning and gradually change its body and environment by changing its thought.

In the sense of making his own character, man is his own maker. He has the free will to think, and his every thought is a tendency in a given direction. One thought does not make a character, but one thought is a tendency toward a character, since once the initial impulse is given, it has a tendency to repeat itself until a habit is formed, and habits make character. Therefore every thought a man thinks has its effect upon his destiny, not only in shaping his present life, but also his future incarnation. Perhaps you were never made aware of how intense a man's thought may be and how immediate is its action upon his physical body. If you are suddenly startled, the effect is instantaneous upon your body, and the entire system may be deranged by the fright.

The majority of men make their physical bodies and their environment unconsciously, but I have known men who have consciously made their bodies over so completely and entirely that their friends did not recognize them afterward. I have seen women change their figures through the power of their thoughts and make them precisely what they desired them to be. Persons who showed the marks of age have brought back the flush of youth, and I have known men and women to prolong their lives far beyond the threescore years and ten that the individuals of our race are supposed to have allotted to them.

LECTURE SIX

COLORS OF THOUGHT VIBRATION

In lecture one we saw that in some of the temples of India there are colored figures and symbols. These played an important part in the occult history of that nation, and depict the forces of man and of nature; but the world has no record left concerning these teachings, and it is only students of mysticism who can read in those colors occult truths. In those Indian temples man is depicted as radiating from himself various colors; but what does that mean to the average mind?

Among the ancient Europeans little was known concerning color. Coming down to more modern history, we find that among the Greeks there were no teachings regarding colors. Greek development ran more particularly to sculpture, arts, architecture and to the use of pigments, rather than to what we call science, and hence they had no knowledge of the nature of vibrations. Passing on to the Romans, we find that they, too, lacked in a large measure any knowledge concerning the nature of color. Seneca seems to be

about the only Roman who wrote anything along
this line, and he only went so far as to show that
the primary colors of the rainbow were the same
as the refraction of sunlight through broken glass,
but he was not able to explain the cause of the
identity of the phenomena. Then passing on to
the Middle Ages, we find that those who had
commenced to investigate this subject of color
from a scientific standpoint, i. e., from the standpoint of light, accepted the theory that all light
is the result of certain colors emitted from ob-
jects. But about 1665 Robert Hook, for the first
time certainly in historic ages, formulated a
theory of wave motions which Christian Huygens,
in 1690, accepted and elaborated and made the
basis of the vibratory or wave theory of light and
color. But the great Newton threw his weight of
opinion with the old emission theory; consequently the wave theory became heterodox and
unpopular, and it was not heard of again for
almost a century. Then once more the scientists
began to talk about the wave theory of light and
of color, and we find the old emission theory dis-
appearing and the wave theory meeting with the
acceptance of the scientific world. This is the
predominating theory of our scientists at present;
but it seems not to have occurred to many of them
that there is an element of truth in both theories
and that by blending parts of the cardinal ideas

of both, an hypothesis might be formulated which would cover all facts and phenomena.

We find a diversity of opinion concerning color among those who study from the standpoint of pigments and those who study from the standpoint of light, as well as some difference of opinion on this subject in each of these several schools. The modern scientist bases his hypothesis upon the wave theory, using for his basis the solar radiation, or the visible so-called white light. And yet he tells you that in point of fact there is no white light, meaning the sum total of all the solar radiation. He tells you that the great emission of light or electrical vibration, whichever it may be, that comes from the sun as a greenish-blue color, is refracted by our atmosphere and manifests itself to our eyes as prismatic colors. But he also says that as the sunlight comes into the world's atmosphere, large proportions of the blue and green rays are withheld by the atmosphere, which has a selective absorption for those colors.

Starting with what must admittedly be largely a hypothetical premise, modern science advances a theory concerning colors based entirely upon such of the solar radiations as reach this earth and are not absorbed by atmospherical conditions, for it does not seem to have occurred to the modern scientist that there is a vibratory force in the earth itself which modifies the solar radiation.

The Occultist has great respect for the indefatigable energy of the modern scientist, and appreciates the painstaking care with which he collects his facts; but he recognizes that the physicist is only working on the plane of effects and hence causes are but guesses with him. These guesses change from decade to decade as new facts are discovered by further research, and hence the Occultist does not feel bound to follow the orthodox theories of any particular decade relative to any branch of knowledge; because he has his own sciences, which have existed for ages, and have been verified by all who have studied along these lines. For this reason we shall not enter too far into the discussion of how near right the modern scientist may be. But the Occultist says this: he does not accept wholly the views of the modern scientist as to primary colors based upon visible solar light.

The accepted prism, you know, consists of the colors red, orange, yellow, green, blue, indigo and violet; and these are considered to be the primary colors. The Occultist says the color you call yellow in point of fact is not yellow, but is the higher rays of the orange, and that the human eye does not record the true primary yellow, because it is beyond the vision of the ordinary eye, even when assisted by mechanical devices. The physicist tells you that your eye cannot detect the ultra violet rays, and that on the other end of the spectrum it cannot follow the lowest vibrations of the red. The Occultist accepts that statement, but adds that you do not detect all the rays or shades of any one of the colors contained even in your spectrum. Again, he differs from the modern physicist in regard to the question of indigo and violet. The Occultist says that indigo and violet are not primary colors, but are only some of the higher and lower rays of the blue, which, in registering themselves upon the human vision, appear as separate colors. Nor does the Occultist agree with those who make a study of pigments—artists and chemists—who consider blue, yellow and red as the primary colors, and that all the other colors are but modifications or blendings of these primary ones. The Occultist says that here also the yellow pigment is not the yellow of the basic vibration, but is merely a modification of the vibration of the orange, and, moreover, that in limiting the primary colors to blue, yellow and red, you leave out entirely the orange and green which are both primary colors. So much, therefore, to show you the lines of divergence between Occultism and the present scientific conception relative to color.

By primary colors, from the standpoint of Occultism, is meant those basic vibrations that appear at the beginning of time, and manifest throughout all planes of nature. Before discussing these, it may be well to enlarge upon some of the points of agreement between modern science and Occultism, which we touched upon in lecture three. First, you will remember that whatever is manifested must have form and color; nothing could manifest if there were a lack of these two qualities, because manifestation means a rate of vibration which parcels or separates a portion of atoms from the mass of matter. Therefore, vibration is the parent of form and color, and manifestation means that there must always exist these two qualities. Take, for example, the flowers; why do they have their various forms? Why do they have their peculiar pigments? Is it not the rate of vibration which determines the size, color and form of the flowers? You remember that when you went to school you were taught that form is the result of vibration, and the fact was illustrated by placing a quantity of fine feathery seed upon a drum head, and then prolonging the notes of a violin over it. The seed gathered into various forms, according to the vibration or sound which was given, and this illustration proved the truth of the teaching. Then you remember the illustration given of the hot poker which changed its color according to

its change in vibration. These illustrations were
given to show that the so-called inanimate things
vibrate, and that their vibrations can be changed
according to the will or desire of man. And now
we will go a step further, and learn something
about the vibrations which determine the form
and color of man himself.

Man, being an individualized manifestation of
nature, must naturally have his form and color.
When I speak of man, I refer to both the physical
and mental man. Place the human body in an
easy position, with feet together, and with arms
at the sides; then draw a line around it, touching
each extreme outer point of the body, and you will
find that the line forms an ovoid. You remember
when we discussed the subjective and the objective minds we found that the two interblended
and ensouled the physical man. These two united
minds not only fill the interstices of the physical
body, and hold together all the physical molecules,
and keep them in place, but also extend beyond
and around the body to the distance of several
inches. If you should draw a line around this
inner or mental man you would find that it, too,
is oval, or egg-shaped, which seems to be the best
form for the highest and largest expression of
individualized consciousness—as witness man,
world, or sun.

Into each center of consciousness flows the mag-

netic force called the life principle, and by reason
of that inflow into all forms there is a constant
pushing out of old atoms and a replacement of
them with new elements. And this is true whether
the form be on the subjective or objective side of
nature. This passing in and out of the atomic
life force, makes a fluidic sphere around each man
and around everything. In electricity we call this
fluidic sphere the electric field; in the sun we call
it the photosphere; around a magnet we call it the
magnetic field or field of attraction. Baron Karl
von Reichenbach, through sensitives, re-discov-
ered in modern times this magnetic field around
men and animals, and even around minerals. This
magnetic field he called "od," or "odic" force.
His discovery is confirmed now by clairvoyants,
by seers, and in France by sensitives under hypnotic influence. Persons from each of these
classes of investigators have seen around each
person, tree and mineral this field of light or
color. This is one reason for that law of physics
which says that no two masses can approach each
other without being mutually affected, because,
being brought into juxtaposition, there is an attraction and repulsion due to the flow of the life
forces, and the exchange of atoms which is constantly taking place between them. There is
essentially nothing in inert matter to attract; but
the inflowing of the life force and the throwing off

of old particles make a change of atoms between masses that are near each other, and they attract or repel according to their similarity or dissimilarity of vibration.

It is the existence of the magnetic field of an animal or a man which enables a dog to follow the scent of either. As a physical, animal body passes over the ground it throws off from itself particles or atoms with each effort or emotion. A certain quantity of these particles is left imprinted upon the earth; and since every individualized consciousness possesses its own distinct odor or perfume—due to its condition of development or rate of vibration—it is not at all difficult for the dog to keep the scent of the creature he is following. The atoms left upon the earth are impregnated with the odor of that person or thing which the dog is able to distinguish from any other.

When we come to the higher centers of consciousness, as in man, we not only have the life force as an element which builds, but we also have a thought force which is constantly manifesting, and by its vibratory flow is modifying, the life force. Each person radiates from himself not only the physical atoms which he has used, and which have lost his vibration, but also the finer forms of matter which go out with his thought force; and therefore there is a continuous stream flowing out from each individual to other centers, and these streams leave their impress upon everything the person thinks about or touches. A sensitive coming in contact with a part of the outflow from a man, can read his character as well as a scientist, by taking up a piece of coal, can tell you its chemical constituency, or its probable age and formation; and this faculty is now called psychometry.

In ancient times, the sphere surrounding man was called the aureola when it encircled his whole body; when it only radiated from his head and shoulders it was called the nimbus. Later, this magnetic field in either aspect was called the aura by Western Occultists, while in the East it was called the sacred Auric Egg. The ancient masters of art always represented their saints with a nimbus about their heads and were accustomed to paint their most divine characters as surrounded by an aureola. In the pictures of Christ there is a radiation from the entire body, while in those of his disciples there is usually but the nimbus to be seen. And these old painters were right in their conceptions; they were sensitives and either had the intuitive knowledge of an occult fact, or they were clairvoyants and saw that according to the development of the ego was the extent of its emanations. The Occultist says that in the ordinary man this radiation extends from two to six inches from the body; but as man develops in thought, power and capacity to draw into himself cosmic forces, his radiations expand until they may extend from six inches to several feet outward.

This aura is one of the chief causes for the unaccountable likes and dislikes that we have for persons whom we meet; for, if one is at all sensitive, one can feel very distinctly the auras one comes in contact with. If we meet with a person whose vibrations are very much higher than our own, we will be likely to either almost worship that person or dislike him for being so far in advance of us. We will be greatly disturbed by the higher vibrations proceeding from him, which will very likely call forth all the good in us, or bring all the sediment in our nature to the surface. Knowing this, and being sensitive to these sudden likes and dislikes for persons, you may save yourself much discomfort by keeping a good distance between yourselves and those who disturb you. A distance of three or four feet will be sufficient to prevent you from feeling so plainly the vibratory force of another.

This aura will also account for the great depletion that many persons feel when they come in contact with other persons; for it is very true that there are human sponges who, unconsciously perhaps, maintain their own lives by drawing all the magnetic force or life they can get from others. This is what the Occultist calls vampirization. You may have observed that invalids are most anxious to have young, strong people about them. They will often take the hand of a healthy person and hold it for hours, if they are permitted to. It is pleasant for the invalid, but quite trying sometimes for the visitor, because with the blending of the auras the magnetic force flows from the stronger to the weaker. Old people are very fond of children, and often insist upon sleeping with them. This is very dangerous for the child, because of the demagnetization which must always follow so doing.

There are several ways by which you may save yourselves from being demagnetized by others. The first is to spend much of your time alone. Another is by declaring positiveness for yourself and by keeping your mind on your own magnetism, and thus retain it within your own body. Again, you may save yourself considerably by letting your feet touch each other lightly, and by clasping your hands together when you are sitting near other persons; this is a means of closing your circuit and preventing your magnetism from flowing out. In the last-mentioned practice it is not alone the physical act of closing your circuit, but the mental attitude you take at that time which protects you from vampirization.

The size and color of the human aura changes according to the intensity and quality of the thought. We have seen that all vibration is either the direct or indirect result of thought; and this is true from the first Divine impulse down to every thought of man. It can be demonstrated in a number of ways. Telepathy, which I believe scientists now accept as a fact, is the transmission of thought or vibratory force from the mind of one person to that of another without the use of material signs, using as the medium of communication the ether or Universal Consciousness. If there is a vibration or emanation that goes forth from you every time you think, and it passes to the point it is sent, then it is reasonable to suppose that according to the intensity of the thought is the emanation projected. If you sit quietly daydreaming, or thinking in an indefinite, incoherent manner, the emanation does not proceed far from you; but if your thought is definite and intense, then its vibration must proceed according to its own intensity. By intense thinking I do not mean that you should clench your fist, nor corrugate your brow while doing it; but I mean that your thought must be clearly held in mind and distinctly sent forth.

I understand that Dr. Baraduct, a French physician, has invented a disk so delicately sensitized that it registers the vibrations of a human being brought in contact with it. If an angry man puts forth his hand toward the dial, the needle on it immediately registers the intensity of his vibrations. If the opposite hand of the same man is extended, the dial immediately shows the difference in vibrations between the positive and negative sides of his body. When a clear, distinct thinker tests the machine, there is a greater number registered upon the dial than when a negative person tests it, and thus we are fortunate in having a recently invented mechanical instrument which proves the claims of Occultism concerning the vibratory emanations from the human body.

The intensity of the thought determines the size of the aura, and the quality of the thought determines its color. For example, you may have an intense vibration of a low color, which would cause your emanation to project for three or more feet from you, or you might have an intense thought of a higher nature which would reach the same distance. Its size would depend upon its intensity, but its color would be determined by its quality or rate of vibration, or its moral and intelligent degree of excellence.

According to the Occult system in reference to mind or man, the spectrum, as applied to this particular planet, would include what is generally known as the absence of color at one end and the synthesis of color at the other, or black and white.

But because neither of these has a practical bearing upon this course of lectures—nor will it have in your lives at this point in your evolution—I shall omit them from this course. Both colors indicate abnormal conditions of mind, and we do not desire to waste our time studying the abnormal. The Occultist says that red, orange, green, blue and yellow are the normal primary colors, and can be seen and known upon each inner plane of being according to the development of the investigator. The ordinarily developed person cannot see the pure yellow ray with his physical eyes any more than the ordinary American can see the many delicate colors in an Indian shawl that the specialized vision of an expert can distinguish.

The inner man, usually called the soul or ego, the real man, always has a color as distinctly his own as has the outside man. Each individual has his particular color according to his quality of thought, character and development. During his first incarnation on the earth the normal color of the subjective mind was yellow or blue, and the natural color of the objective mind was green; therefore, when these two first came together, and united as one mind, and incarnated in a human body, the combined colors became a greenish blue or greenish yellow. This very quickly changed to lower rates of vibration, because sensation immediately commenced to manifest in the place of reason, in the newly incarnated man. The green predominated over the yellow or blue because the latter were the product of the subjective side of life, and the green was the product of the objective side which was stronger upon its own plane of development. But even these combination color vibrations were lost through the excitation of the emotional nature, which came quickly into the ascendency in man's nature. This was due to the great desire for the physical enjoyments of life, for in those days man was in his absolutely normal, animal condition. He had a new body, had not put into action causes which reacted upon it, and his power of thinking was limited, and therefore not likely to have much influence on his body during those first incarnations. So there was nothing for man at that time but the mere physical enjoyment of existence.

Before we take up the study of the emotional nature and its colors, it may be well to examine that force which built man's physical form, and which builds all physical forms—the force we call "life." This force manifests as orange vibration. If life is a force, if it is something, then it must have a rate of vibration of its own to distinguish it from everything else in the universe. We speak of the Gulf Stream. It is a current of water which vibrates at a higher rate than the body of water

through which it flows, and we call this current
of water the Gulf Stream to distinguish it from
the rest of the ocean. So in this great sea of
consciousness there are certain definite and distinct currents of force which play very important
parts in man's evolution, and that which we call
"life" is one of them. I cannot prove this statement to you because of the limitation of your
vision, but you can prove it for yourself—as you
can prove every other statement I shall make in
these lectures—if you develop to that point where
your inner senses permit you to function upon
that plane of existence where forces are visible
as forces, as causes, and not as effects or
phenomena.

On this physical plane you see life as form; on
the subjective or mental side you see life manifesting as a separate and distinct thing which is
building the form you see with your physical
eyes. Seeing life on the subjective side, it is an
orange color, or a force which vibrates as orange,
sweeping into everything and giving vitality to
all forms. All physical bodies have this vital
force manifesting in them according to the capacity of each to express it. You do not see the
orange force permeating the invalid to the same
extent that it does an athlete, because the invalid
cannot express it so well. And now that you
understand something about the force which

fashions and preserves the physical body, let us turn to man himself and study the other forces expressed in him.

The lowest force in psychic man is that which we designate as his distinct animal propensities, and these are red in their manifestation or vibration. You remember we found the four cardinal emotions upon which all the other human emotions were based, and the first three of these were red; therefore, when the animal nature is in the ascendency in man, when it dominates the intellectual side of his nature, the red vibrations become the dominating ones and permeate the entire man and his aura. If you strike a tuning fork upon the table, the sound produced is the vibration which emanates from that tuning fork. If you put a weight upon the fork the sound ceases, because the low rate of vibration which you bring in contact with the tuning fork causes its vibrations to be lowered, and finally to cease; thus the vibrations of the weight overcome those of the tuning fork. It is the same with thought; when the animal nature becomes intense it gives its lowering vibrations to every part of the man, and consequently the intellectual nature ceases its activity for the time being, and takes the color of the dominating emotion. When the emotional nature is in the ascendency, man's color is red, and according to the intensity of his emotions is the color intensified; but if he struggles to control his emotions there will be a change of colors in his aura.

In the course of time man's lower intellectual nature began to be more prominent, and when his emotions were not over-stimulated it began to be something of a factor in his life; and as time went on what was originally the red in the psychic man, and the orange of his body, became tinged with the green of his objective mentality, and then he had the three colors blended, which gave him a brown vibration. This color, unfortunately, indicates the condition of the mass of men at the present day, because they have not developed beyond that point. The intellectual side of man is very weak as yet; even the objective mind is not well individualized, and as for the subjective mind, it is not active in one person in a thousand.

After many centuries some men, for one reason or another, began to control their emotions somewhat. This may have been brought about by laws being enacted which said: If a person gives sway to his emotions, and kills another, or becomes too avaricious, and robs his fellow man, he shall be punished. Or it may have been because social life required the suppression of the emotions at times. As man began to control more and more his emotional nature, the green vibrations became more prominent. First in its deeper shades—

which indicate intense selfishness—and subsequently in its lighter shades, indicating individualization.

Green is the color of the objective mind of man when he first begins to individualize as a permanent center of consciousness in Deity. It is the color of the manifested, lower, intellectual nature which is sometimes called the brain consciousness. Self-consciousness in the growing man was necessarily an evolutionary step; and when man, for his own purposes and his own interests, began to use his intellect even on a low plane, he began to control his emotional nature. This in itself helped to strengthen his intellectual nature and made his emotions more or less subservient to it. Green vibrations are desirable because no soul can mount very high in its evolution unless it becomes properly individualized. Then will come the time when our subjective minds, or the diviner portion of our natures, will fight for the ascendency as the lower intellectual is now fighting the emotional nature. At that time the original color of the subjective mind will begin to manifest itself and the blue vibrations will commence to tinge the inner man. At first there will be but occasional flashes of the blue in his aura; later, it will become suffused with the blue vibration.

Raising the vibrations of the developing man is a slow process. Where his higher intellect and intuition begin to manifest, and where reason commences to overpower desire, there is the battle ground for the objective and subjective minds. This is where most of the progressive men and women are to-day; and if you were clairvoyant, you could see the auras changing from green to blue, with often a flash of red, and then back again to green, or perhaps to purple, a combination of the blue and red. I know of no better comparison than to liken the progressive inner man, in his appearance, to an electric fountain. One moment you may see the fountain all blue, at another green and blue mingling; then perhaps it will change to purple, with now and again a flash of red, or with red suffusing the whole. So man, according to his thought, is always radiating these beautiful colors which are in each human soul or mind.

In the course of time, when his spiritual nature becomes awakened and his intuition becomes active, the yellow vibrations begin to interblend with the blue. You will see the well-developed man possessed of all the colors, properly regulated and controlled. The lower vibrations, the red, will then appear as a beautiful rose pink, and will be seen more particularly about that portion of the body where the generative organs are located. The orange vibration will suffuse the entire body. The green will be the individualizing band outlining the body, and the blue and yellow will blend and extend beyond the green, forming the outer border of the aura.

There are two classes of these colors which may be designated as positive and negative. There is the positive yellow and the negative yellow, the positive green and the negative green. And when you see man's aura composed of negative colors you may know that the negative side of his nature is dominant. A man may be negatively good, and be neither wise nor strong. He may seem to control his objective mind and you may believe him to be a well-developed man, when really his objective mind is but a poor vehicle for his subjective mind. Or you may find persons with the negative blue and yellow vibrations, those whose intuitional natures are only partially awakened, but who have not the force aspect; neither has the higher intelligence become active in them. A person may be negatively good because he has not been tempted in this life to be otherwise; his environment may have been such as to guard him against temptation, and his nature being negative, he had not the desire to overcome. Some time in some life he must be tempted and learn to be positively good before he becomes a perfected ego.

There is a practical side to this lecture, as there has been to all the other lectures of this course.

According to your knowledge of these forces or vibrations, and according to the intensity of your thought, will you have the power to use the Occult forces of nature, and become conscious upon other than the material plane, and to put yourself in touch with certain cosmic currents or forces. For illustration: A man with an emotional nature goes to the theater. There is a cry of "Fire!" and a wave of fear sweeps over the audience. Every mind in the house has become attached to the red cosmic current of fear. Having tapped this great current, waves of fear come into every center of consciousness in that house, and the emotional man loses his reason and rushes like a maddened brute to save himself, regardless of everyone else. He tramples upon women and children, and fights like a wild animal to liberate his body from the struggling mass of human beings around him. There may or may not be a fire, but this man has connected his objective mind, through thought, with this current of fear, does not control the emotion as it sweeps over him, and you see the result.

These cosmic currents which surround our earth correspond in color and rate of vibration to each of the colors in the aura of men and animals; and all living creatures use these currents, either consciously or unconsciously. When man learns to vibrate harmoniously with the color or cosmic current he desires to use, then his development will be much more rapid than when he uses the currents, as the animals do, unconsciously and without a knowledge of what he is doing. It is according to the color of a man's vibrations that he connects himself with these cosmic forces; and some of the lower forces bring disaster to him when he uses them. Take the current of fear for example. If a man is constantly fearing something, or someone, he thus connects himself with the current of fear, and it constantly plays upon him. He never can gain success in anything he undertakes until he raises his vibrations above this current, and in this way disconnects himself from it. It is indeed of the most importance that man should learn to control his thoughts and his vibrations.

There are also different planes of consciousness, and it is according to the rate of man's vibration that he can function upon them. As a man may be able to see no color but red, because his optic nerves are at so low a rate of vibration that they cannot record any color of a higher rate, so some men have a much broader apprehension of the laws of life than other men, because their vibrations are high enough to permit vibrations coming from other and higher planes to impinge upon their consciousness. A genius is a man whose consciousness has become expanded through his evolution until he can contact more planes of cosmic consciousness than other men. You remember the lines,

> "A primrose by a river's brim
> A yellow primrose was to him,
> And it was nothing more."

One man sees in a primrose nothing more nor less than a vegetable growth; another thinks what a pretty yellow flower; still another sees in that same primrose the secrets of the Universe; he sees in that flower the vibratory effect of the Divine Idea—that God has geometrized, as the scholars of Pythagoras were accustomed to say.

There are forty-nine states of consciousness, but the minds of average men only function upon ten or twelve. There are a great many doors to knowledge, which we may open if we will; but if we continue to think in the lower states of consciousness, and never rise above them in aspiration, these other doors will remain forever shut to us. If we always live in the cellar of our house we will never see God's sunlight streaming into our upper rooms. The sun shines, but not for us because we will not go where it can reach us.

All the world's great teachers have substantially taught the same rules for conduct and morality. Ethics is not founded on police regulations nor sentiments of moralists, but is established on the immutable laws of nature. "Love your enemies" was one of the precepts taught by Jesus, and it has puzzled many of his followers to find the reason for the teaching. Many persons think, if they do not say: What sense is there in loving one's enemies? This precept has a purely scientific basis. Love is not an indefinite sentiment, it is something real; it is the highest and greatest dynamic force on this planet, and is one that manifests on all planes. Since it is a force, it is something we can feel on this plane of effects and see on the mental plane, if we are able to function on that plane. When pure love is sent forth from the subjective mind, it manifests as a constructive force, having its own particular high yellow rate of vibration. Anger being an emotion, and proceeding from the objective mind of man, vibrates at a lower rate, which is red. A person who hates you—an enemy—sends a red current of thought toward you; but if you send loving thoughts in return, you are projecting a yellow rate of vibration which is infinitely higher and more forceful than the red, and the yellow vibration deflects the lower vibration so that it never reaches you.

The higher rates of vibration will protect you

from harm, and if you live according to ethical principles, a high quality of thought or vibration is attained. When we come to consider Spiritual Forces, we shall see how, by the control of our thoughts, we can use the cosmic forces.

LECTURE SEVEN

ALL religions invent modes whereby the mind of man is directed to Deity. In the Eastern philosophy these modes are called Yoga, and are supposed to be methods of yoking the individual mind to the Universal Consciousness. There are two principal kinds of yoga, which may be described as mental and as physical. The first is a process of meditation, by which the individual mind is brought into closer relationship with the Universal Consciousness; the second or physical yoga, is of various kinds, and includes methods of artificial breathings and unusual and unnatural postures of the body. These postures and breathings are for the purpose of drawing into the physical body certain forces which develop psychic powers. It is believed by those who practice them that a step nearer Deity is gained by so doing; but in point of fact only certain psychic centers in the physical body are awakened, which enable these persons to function upon the first plane beyond the material. The ecstatic conditions into which the Yogi are often thrown by indulging in these practices are not spiritual states of consciousness, as many persons believe, but are entirely due to paroxysms of emotion to which they yield, and which are disastrous to those who indulge in them.

Another system devised for the purpose of relating the individual consciousness to the Universal Consciousness is ritualism, and we find this method almost, if not quite, perfected in the East. In the elaborate ceremonials of Brahminism and Buddhism there is as complete a ritual as exists. In Buddhistic ritualism there are various steps, from the worship of the Supreme in meditation, to the attempt to reach and propitiate the intermediate forces, gods or devas.

In Judaism we find again a great system of ritualism, which is second only to that of Buddhism; but the ritualism of Judaism was established for a material people, it used material processes for carrying out its ritual and never reached the point where it operated upon mental lines. For example, in Judaism we find the cutting of the throats of animals and the flowing of blood. This was a sacrificial rite and was supposed to attract the attention of the Deity, through His love for the shedding of blood, to propitiate Him, and induce Him to give to whomever made this sacrifice something of much more value than were the animals slaughtered. It was not for the sake of spirituality that these rites were performed, but for material gain only.

And then came Christianity, represented in the West by the two great sects, Catholicism on the one hand, and Protestantism on the other. These also use a process to relate the individual consciousness to the Universal, which is called prayer or petition. The ritual in Catholicism is on the same general lines as in Buddhism, because many of its rites were obtained from Buddhism. For example, there are three forms of prayer in Catholicism: the Latria, or prayer direct to Deity; Hyperdulia, or prayer to Deity through the intercession of the saints or the Virgin Mary, and the Doulia, or prayer to a special patron saint; in Protestantism the prayer is made directly to Jehovah. Whether we consider the old religions of the world, or the most modern, each has invented a process for relating the mind back to the Universal Consciousness, and all these rites are for one purpose—personal gain.

Some of you may be shocked by this declaration, but upon close analysis you will find it true. In Buddhism the object of relating the individual mind to the Universal Consciousness is the hope for liberation from rebirth; it is purely a question of benefit to the individual. In Judaism a bargain between the individual and the Universal was made. In return for prayers and praise and sacrifices, God was supposed to give men things which they wanted. In Catholicism, in exchange for prayers and chanting, God gave men mental or spiritual qualities and personal salvation; but they, too, can obtain material things by doing a Novena. This last process of prayer is not made to God direct, but to Saint Anthony, and if the conditions required by this Saint are all fulfilled, the prayer is answered. In Protestantism the prayer may be for personal health, for a person going to sea, or for the kingdom of heaven, or for something else—it all comes back to a matter of personal benefit.

The Christian and Mental Scientists have adopted from the Orient a process of meditation called "going into the silence." This attitude of mind is for the purpose of harmonizing the individual mind with the Universal, in order that the individual may receive thoughts and things that it desires, and is a form of prayer along more rational and scientific lines. Occultism, too, has its processes for the purpose of relating the individual mind to the Universal Consciousness, in order that it may draw such spiritual, mental and material things as the individual needs or wants.

The question arises, how can this relation be brought about, because we all need something spiritual, mental or material, and in our hearts we wish to know how to use our minds in order to obtain the qualities or things desired. The three working tools or methods of mind that the Occultist takes for the purpose of connecting his consciousness with the Universal, are the processes known as Meditation, Creation and Concentration.

We have spoken repeatedly of mind, and now we will say something about thought. Thought is the product of mind; it is a rate of vibration sent forth from mind, and therefore is force. This thought force is continually being used or misused, because to live is to think, either rightly or wrongly, with the objective or subjective mind. Thought, per se, is neither good nor bad, but, like any other force, the use of it determines its character. Electricity is a force, and can be used constructively to dissipate disease and to prolong life, or it can be used to destroy life, as the State of New York destroys the lives of criminals at Sing Sing.

Thought has one chief characteristic, I might almost say but one characteristic, and that is vibration. From this standpoint we may divide thought into two general classes, that of the positive and negative. Positive thought is a high rate of vibration sent forth from the mind, and negative thought is a low rate of vibration.

You remember that the will is the positive side of the subjective mind, and corresponds to the desire or the positive side of the objective mind. The will plays a very important part in human affairs, whether it becomes active in the subjective mind as will power, or whether it operates in the objective mind as desire. In connection with thought the will has three functions:

First. It determines the nature of the thought sent forth from the mind, whether it be constructive or destructive.

Second. Will determines the intensity of the thought, whether it shall vibrate at a high rate and travel with great rapidity, or whether it shall proceed at a low rate, and reach but a short distance. In other words, the will determines whether the thought shall be positive or negative.

Third. Will determines the direction of thought; ·that is, the person, place or thing to which it shall be sent and how long it shall remain in each place.

Knowing the functions of this tremendous force, which in its higher aspects is latent in most persons, you can see how essential it is that it should be awakened; for, like the muscles of the body, will grows stronger with use. It is left with each of us to determine whether we shall remain infirm of purpose and weak in will, or awaken, and arouse this force and use it for our upbuilding. Without the activity of will no one can hope to become an Occultist, because his mental force is to him what the engine is to the engineer.

The first mental mode to cultivate in order that the mind may draw to itself whatever it desires is Philosophical Meditation. (I use the word philosophical as qualifying this state of mind, because there are various other modes of so-called meditation.)

Philosophical meditation is a receptive condition of mind, assumed for the purpose of receiving from Deity knowledge concerning a selected subject.

In order to understand more fully the elements which compose this kind of meditation, we will analyze them. The first condition of mind is a receptive one. In using the word "receptive" I do not mean negative. Never, under any circumstances, permit yourself to be in a negative condition, because the moment you become negative you become subject to malevolent subjective entities and influences which may control or obsess you and perhaps dominate your mind throughout this life.

The Occultist insists most vehemently that the passive negative meditation taught by many schools in the Orient as well as in the Occident is most harmful to the ego. Since immortality means the preservation of the individual consciousness, a perfect individualization can come

only through the continued effort to remain in a
positive condition of mind. It therefore follows
that to remain negative is detrimental to one's
evolution. Negativeness also has its effects upon
the physical body by its reflex action producing
sickness and often dissolution. If there is one
idea that will be emphasized more than another
during this course of lectures it will be the necessity of being mentally positive. Stability is the
result of positiveness and the Biblical assertion
is true in Occultism as in everything else that:
"unstable as water thou shalt not excel."

A receptive condition of mind is the same
mental condition that you are now in. A quiet,
listening, expectant attitude; not intense but waiting, giving positive attention to what I am saying
while your bodies are in a relaxed but comfortable
position. No one could control any mind in this
room at this moment because each one is positive
and is in an active instead of a passive condition.

Having placed yourself in this receptive condition you desire to receive knowledge. Knowledge
is the second element in our definition, and is all
that you can receive through meditation; since
qualities or things are brought through other
modes of mind.

Now direct your demand or prayer to the Universal Consciousness—not to an individual, for
there must be no intermediary; prayer must be

directed to Deity as in the highest form of Christianity. You go into meditation for the purpose of receiving knowledge from the highest source of knowledge, and this is the third element in our definition.

To demand scientifically and well from Deity is a very hard thing to do unless you have entirely outgrown the idea of an anthropomorphic God, because at first it seems difficult to address Universal Consciousness. It may seem that your demand or prayer has gone into space somewhere to diffuse itself throughout the great Consciousness. It may be of help to you to consider the Universal Consciousness as another individual mind near you that you may speak to as you would to another person. Or better still, you may picture it as a golden sun or center of vibrating light within your own heart—for the heart center is one of the chief points of contact between the individual and the Universal mind.

I wish to impress upon your mind the thought of your nearness to this Universal Consciousness. Many persons feel so far away from God and when they think of Deity at all they think of It as a being somewhere far away in space. God is difficult to reach only because you make it so with your wrong conceptions of your separateness from Him. You should take the great Consciousness into every thought and act of life; whisper to It in the darkness of the night and It will hear and answer you. See It in a mental picture of golden yellow light and It will fill your body with Its uplifting vibrations. Depend upon It, instead of persons and things, to bring you what you need and your demands will never fail to be met.

There are two reasons why your demands should be made of the Universal Consciousness. First, because if you do not address your demands to the Highest your objective mind will immediately assert itself and assume the responsibility of answering you. It will pretend to be God and give you back something purporting to be the particular knowledge you demanded. By making your demand direct to Deity it has a tendency to prevent the action of the lower objective mind. It is only a tendency, however, and nothing but perfect self-control will ever fully prevent the attempted intervention by the objective mind.

The second reason for addressing your demand to the Supreme Consciousness, as if it were another mind, is that you thereby have a tendency to cut off communication with all other individual minds who are thinking along the same general line with yourself; otherwise you may get into a current of thought and be as likely to get wrong thoughts as right ones.

Many persons "go into the silence," or try to

meditate by sitting and waiting for any thought to come to them. In this way they receive any impressions that may sweep into their minds, believing such impressions are Divine Inspiration. But all this is not Philosophical Meditation and cannot possibly bring the good you desire. The proper way to meditate is to get your subject before going into meditation and then ask for knowledge concerning it and wait patiently for your impression. It is absolutely necessary that you should have a concrete subject because concreteness is the secret of success along mental as well as along all other lines. The subject for meditation may be anything concerning which you desire knowledge. It may be knowledge pertaining to any plane of being, the Spiritual, Mental, or Physical; but it must be concrete.

The majority of persons do not think, they merely dream. You often hear the remark, "A penny for your thoughts," and the reply usually comes, "Why, really I don't know what I was thinking about." People think they think, but in point of fact they jump from subject to subject as a bird flits from one limb of a tree to another. There is no logical sequence to their thought, there is no continuity. Many persons think of words, not of concepts or of concrete mental things; and this is sometimes true even with persons who are called scientific. What concept do

most persons have of Love, Force, Mind, Thought?
If these words mean anything then these are
things.   It is possible to have thoughts without
words and this kind of thinking is mental picture
making, or concrete thought, which is the real,
creative thought. Your careless thinking has very
little or no results, while your concrete thoughts
have absolute, mathematical results.

Returning to the subject of meditation we
should first consider the best time for this practice, for in the beginning it is better to have a
definite time set apart for it—after awhile you
will be able to meditate at any time or place. The
early morning hours are the best for meditation
because at that time great forces of nature are
sweeping through you and through that part of
the world where the sun is beginning to shine.
At that time all your own magnetic forces have
been drawn back to you during the previous sleep
and you have not as yet been drawn into the
world's thought. If you can devote some time to
meditation before you rise you will get the best
results; besides you will consciously bring yourself into a closer relationship with Deity and
thus establish harmony for yourself, which will
better enable you to undertake the duties of the
day.

When you demand knowledge from the Universal Consciousness there go forth from you,

according to the intensity of your thought, many little magnetic lines into the ether. These lines look like blue rays of light and connect you with the person or thing which will be the best instrument to answer your demand. Sometimes this instrument is another ego who consciously through telepathy sends you an answer to your question. Or perhaps Deity may use a material agency and connect you with a treatise on the subject on which you desire information; or you may have an invitation to attend a lecture which would give you the knowledge you have demanded.

There are various ways through which your demand may be met and Deity provides the best way for you according to your development and ability to receive at that time. It is true the answer does not always come immediately after the demand is made, and you may continue to demand for a day, a week or a month before it comes. The concreteness and intensity of your thought determine the promptness of the response. And if there should be a delay it will be through no fault of the Universal Consciousness or of the law of supply and demand, any more than an error in your calculations would prove wrong a rule in mathematics. The fault will be in yourself; because you do not think clearly enough or hold your thought picture sufficiently long. If you will persistently follow the rules given in this lecture, your impressions will always come in time for you to use them.

Most beginners make their demand of Deity and then go and ask some person for advice and opinions along that particular line. As a consequence several answers are received and none may be right because Deity did not make the connections. The impatient beginner did not wait for Deity to make his connections, but ran around and made them himself, and perhaps long after he has acted upon his erroneous information the correct answer will come from Deity.

Here are some rules which may help you in your work:

First. Mistrust all *immediate* answers; because the chances are that when your reply comes at once, your objective mind is speaking to you. In the beginning of your Philosophical Meditations you have not had sufficient practice to enable you always to determine the difference between the impressions from your own objective mind and those from Deity, and so it is well to repeat the question at each period of meditation for several days in succession.

Second. Examine the answer closely when it comes in the form of words, and consider it well because the objective mind invariably expresses itself in words and sometimes in a long dissertation. The Universal Consciousness usually conveys the answer to your mind in an impression or conviction.

Third. Test the answer by your reason until your intuition has become fully awakened and can tell you where the answer came from. For example, suppose you ask if it is best for you to do a certain thing and the answer comes back "yes," and shocks your sense of justice or of truth, of expediency or of probability. Sit in judgment upon it with your reason until your intuition is awakened and do not act hastily.

Fourth. You will find that Deity will usually answer your question at an unexpected moment, when your objective mind is off guard. By receiving an answer at such a time you get it uncolored by your objective mind or desire.

If you will remember these four suggestions or tests and apply them to your work in Philosophical Meditation you will receive the knowledge you desire; and if mistakes should be made in the beginning, your implicit trust in Deity will render such mistakes harmless and ultimately turn them to good.

The second mode of mind is Creation. Thought creation is the imaging or putting into concrete form a selected subject. By concrete form is meant a mental picture of the selected subject invested with all the qualities of that subject in its natural state. Mental creation will bring you any quality or any thing you want, except knowledge, which comes through meditation. Imagination is not fancy; it is the image-making faculty which is used for the purpose of making a concrete picture of the thing we desire. Do you want love? What is love? If you are going to create a thing you must have a concrete picture of it. Love is a force. Being a force it must have a rate of vibration, and having a rate of vibration it must have a color. Therefore when you picture love you must picture it according to your highest conception of what that force would be, and the color of the highest force upon this planet is yellow.

If it is Divine love you want, see yourself standing in a flood of this golden vibrating force; see It bathing you in Its rays, penetrating every part and particle of your being till your body and you vibrate in response to It, and until the atmosphere around you pulsates and throbs with Its golden glow. If you desire to send love to another, picture the Universal Love flowing into yourself and then see it passing from your heart's center as a golden stream flowing outward till it reaches the heart to which it is sent. Some of your own being will enter and warm the heart of the one to whom you send that love force, and you will have the joy that comes through loving and being loved. If you wish to demonstrate love from another, see that golden current of force flowing from that other person to you.

If you wish to work upon the mental plane, if you wish to demand a greater mentality, picture the blue Cosmic Force flowing into you. Picture yourself as suffused with this blue force until your whole being vibrates with it. Let it magnetize your brain and thrill you through and through with its uplifting force. After a demonstration of this kind you will feel capable of accomplishing any mental undertaking. Do not deceive yourself into the belief that one treatment with this blue Cosmic Force will make of you a genius, because it will not. But constant treatments of this kind will gradually increase your mental power, which you can direct into any channel you desire, and the picture you make creates the center or matrix into which the Universal Consciousness can bring that which you demand.

On the material plane the same picture-making faculty is used. Do you want to build up a fine law practice? Then picture your clients coming in large numbers to your office, engaging your services and paying you liberally—this last part of the picture is an essential portion of the whole. Do you wish to develop a business? Then see crowds of people coming and waiting for you to serve them. But good, bad and indifferent business will come unless you limit your creation to a certain class; then that kind or class of business which you have created will come. But while you are waiting for your creations to materialize, for your demands to be met, you should do cheerfully and faithfully such duties as are presented to you to do. In this way you will co-operate with the Supreme because you will never know till a duty is done what good may come to you from doing that duty well.

Do you want money? Then make a concrete picture of the amount you want—say a one-hundred-dollar bill; or if you do not want your money all of one denomination picture a sufficient number of bills, of the denomination you want, to make the amount you desire. But in any event make a picture of a definite amount and after making it, hold to it till it stands out as distinct as though it had materialized and you could see it before you. Then say to the Universal Consciousness, "Give me this creation," and repeat this demand day after day and many times a day if you want to. You can do this instead of dreaming or reading the signs in the street cars, etc. The concreteness of your picture makes your creation a mental reality and the more tenaciously you hold to the mental creation the sooner will the material reality come. Creative thought is always in pictures. This is true from a higher or a lower viewpoint. For example: the Universe

is the materialization of the Divine Idea; the
Spiritual plane received the impress of the Divine
Mind when creation commenced and the Planetary
Spirits, seeing the picture, poured into it their
own vibratory force and so worlds were brought
into existence. Everything that is, existed first
on the mental plane, even to the clothes you wear
and the chair you sit on.

Let us further examine the working of the law,
and will take for example the concrete picture of
a bundle of money—one hundred dollars. You
have made a mental picture or image of this
creation and now you are sending your force,
which is simply thought vibrations, into that picture until it becomes clearly defined in the ether
which surrounds your own aura. The clearness
of your thought and the intensity of your picture
make a photograph, as it were, in the Universal
Mind, and this is your matrix or plan. If the
matrix of your thumb nail should be destroyed
you could never have another thumb nail in this
life, but so long as the matrix is there, although
the nail may be for the time being destroyed,
another will grow. And so it is with your mental
matrix, so long as it is not destroyed it will sometime draw to you the material thing pictured.
The constant or frequent vibration which your
thought causes, sets the Universal Consciousness
surrounding you and your picture into action.

Then out from you goes the small magnetic cord
which the Universal Consciousness directs to the
sum of money you have demanded. This money
is somewhere upon the material plane when you
make your demand for it, and the Universal Consciousness directs your demand, with its tiny
magnetic cord attached, to this amount of money.
It is no affair of yours where this one hundred
dollars shall come from. The avenue through
which it may come is for the Universal Consciousness to select, and, being Justice, It will bring it
from the source whence it should come, and no one
will be unjustly treated by the transference of it
to your possession.

That the matrix is a reality and is the image of
a mental thing, is testified to by all Occultists,
seers and good psychics. This testimony was cor-
roborated last week by the press dispatches, which
stated that Doctor Baraduct, of Paris, has now
perfected a photographic plate so sensitive as to
catch the image of thought pictures. The report
of his invention went on to state that a noted
French naturalist was requested to think of, or
image something of his own selection while the
plate was exposed. After the negative was developed, there was the picture of a rare specimen
of eagle which the naturalist declared was the
image he had held in his mind. He had been
studying this unusual bird for some time previous,

and was able to make his mental picture very clear in consequence. The report also stated that many imperfect pictures were taken from the thoughts of other persons. From the general public Dr. Baraduct got the best results from women who were in love. He said they seemed to be able to hold in mind a very clear picture of those they loved. Whether these reports are true or not, I am not prepared to say; but sooner or later physical science will establish this claim of the Occultists.

In making your demands, you must make them of Deity and not of any person. You have no right to use coercive force upon another individual mind; but since everything that exists belongs to Deity—and Deity is the source of your supply—you have a perfect right to demand of It. At this point of our evolution we create mental pictures of things already in existence and draw them to us according to the operation of the law I have just explained. But the time will come in our development when we can image a thing and have the power to draw together the particles necessary to its composition, and create the thing itself. This power is called precipitation, and is really the highest form of creation.

Mental Concentration is the third mode of mind. It is not in its nature creative, but it is the direction of force which hastens the materializa-

tion of creations. Concentration is holding the
mind on one subject to the exclusion of every
other subject. Here, again, you must have a
specific subject to concentrate upon, and it may
be any quality, thought or thing. This mode of
mind is perhaps the most forceful of the three
modes mentioned in this lecture. It is therefore
always an active, positive condition of mind. The
habit of concentration is not acquired in a short
time, but is a matter of growth, a matter of practice. You will be surprised to know that the
average person cannot—or does not, perhaps I
should say—hold his mind for ten consecutive seconds on one subject.

For example, take this creation we last selected,
the bundle of money. Try to hold your mind on
that one-hundred-dollar creation for a moment.
After a few seconds you begin to wonder whether
that creation is really coming, and then you bring
your mind back to your subject, and look at that
mental picture for another couple of seconds.
Then you suddenly remember that there is a magnetic cord attached to each demand that goes forth
from you, and you wonder if that magnetic cord is
all right; then you try to see the cord and the
first thing you know you have lost sight of the
money, and are creating a magnetic cord attach-
ment to your demand. Suddenly you become conscious that your mind is wandering and you won-

der if you are concentrating right; and thus your thoughts skip from one thing to another and you learn by experience that concentration is gained only by patient and constant practice.

Knowing something about the law of periodicity, which makes and unmakes habits, you may take advantage of it in learning how to concentrate. Some suggestions may be helpful to you in acquiring this art of concentration and making it a habit of thought. Select an hour in the morning, or take a part of the same hour that you give to meditation; give the first ten or twenty minues to meditation and the remainder of the time to concentration. If this practice is persisted in for several days in succession you will find your concentration becoming easier, because the law of periodicity will be operating with you; and the impetus thus given to concentration soon makes the practice a habit of mind.

Look at your mental creation quietly, but intensely. Think of the picture—say the money—for about twenty minutes. Concentration means looking at your picture. It is not very hard work to sit and look at one hundred dollars; indeed, it can be made a very pleasant thing to do, if you realize that it is yours. Concentration should always be a pleasant exercise of will, a quiet but positive condition of mind. Let the mind rest entirely upon your mental picture and claim it by saying or thinking "that is mine, because I have created it."

Many persons make hard work of trying to concentrate. This is a mistaken waste of physical force. When you see a pretty flower and look at it admiringly, you are thinking of that flower and are concentrating upon it, because for the moment you are thinking of it to the exclusion of everything else. When you go to the theater, and become absorbed by the acting, you are concentrating upon the acting. With most persons, in trying to concentrate, the tendency is to imagine that they are placing themselves in a false or unnatural condition of mind; they feel that they are going to do something they have never done before, or something they are not accustomed to do. Perhaps they will shut their teeth together, and whisper tragically, "Now I am going to concentrate," and then, with clenched fists and corrugated brows, they knot their muscles till the perspiration starts, and the breath comes hard and fast. Dismiss the mistaken idea, for that is an artificial condition of mind. Concentration is not a fiery ordeal; it is a natural and a pleasant recreation, or should be.

Put your body in an easy position, and whenever your attention is attracted to your body you may know it is getting tense; then relax and forget about it, because all your force is needed in looking at your picture. But after a while your mind may grow tired of looking at any particular form. For instance, in concentrating on that bundle of money, you may not be tired of the money, or of the concentration, but you may become tired of that particular form of picture. If you have been looking at greenbacks, change your picture to gold or silver for a while. It does not matter what kind of money you have, so long as you get the amount you desire. In this way, you see, your matrix is not destroyed, but only the form of your picture is changed. Another very good aid to concentration is to form the habit of concentrating your thoughts upon everything you do in your daily life. If you are tying your shoe, think of tying that shoe until it is tied; do not be tying your shoe and trying to read a newspaper at the same time. If it is dressing for dinner, think of your dressing; do not be dressing and practicing a solo at the same time. This regular practice of concentration will greatly quicken your power, and enable you to do thoroughly and speedily everything you undertake. The successful men of the world are those who have practiced, and have acquired, the art of concentrating upon special lines.

Hundreds of Mental Scientists and Christian Scientists of our time, and the Occultists throughout the Ages, have demonstrated the truths given in this lecture. You may believe these principles, but you will never know them until you demonstrate them for yourself. If you persist in practicing the rules given, you can draw to yourselves anything you care to picture. If you desire success, social position, any spiritual, mental or physical thing, it can be gained by simply creating and holding the picture in your mind. It makes no difference whether the thing you create is good for you to have, or whether you use or misuse it after you get it, you will get whatever you clearly picture. If you want a thousand dollars for the purpose of helping a poor family, or to hire a man to murder another, it makes no difference with the operation of the law. Your demand will be met if you make your picture of the thousand dollars. But if you misuse your powers or direct your forces to the detriment of another, you must take the consequences and these are very direful, because the law of Justice acts much more quickly upon persons who consciously misuse mental forces than upon those who do wrong in a half-conscious manner.

It is always well to meditate before you create a thing. So many persons are continually creating and demanding things they do not really want. Ask the Supreme Consciousness, God, Father, whatever you choose to call the Great Source, if there is any reason why you should not have the thing you desire; and when the impression comes, "there is no reason why you should not have it," then make your picture, claim it for your own, and then concentrate upon it until it comes. But suppose you think you would like to go to Europe, and, without meditating upon it, or asking if it is best for you to go, you make a picture of yourself on the steamer with your ticket for Europe. You will go to Europe, but you may be very ill after you get there, or you may be shipwrecked going or coming, or many things may happen to make you miserable on your trip. If you had meditated upon the matter, and asked for the knowledge of what it was best to do, you would have received the impression that it was not best to go at that time. Then had you acted upon that impression, and stayed at home, all these calamities would have been avoided.

LECTURE EIGHT

At this period of our history most people make
the word Occultism synonymous with psychism.
In reality there is a vast difference between the
two. The meaning of the former word you have
heretofore seen, and now it remains for us to examine one of its sub-divisions, which is psychism.
It is very essential that we should know something
about the psychic realm, if for no other reason
than that we may be able to avoid it. It is rather
a dark side of nature; nevertheless, it seems desirable that you should know the truth, though it
may offend and even frighten some of you. The
necessity for this lecture is due, first, to the fact
that people who take up this line of study are, for
this very reason, in a position where they must
contact very closely the psychic realm; and second, that humanity as a whole, in its evolutionary
career, is now beginning to approach the psychic
plane. The psychically advanced members of the
human race have contacted it already, much to the
detriment of some of them, and for these reasons

it is the imperative duty of someone who knows the facts of nature to reveal them, even though the revelation should excite the incredulity and scorn of the ignorant, and possibly the enmity of those who, in their researches, have contacted the psychic side, and have fallen under its deceptive influence.

Those of you who are familiar with Bulwer's writings know that there is a vein of mysticism running through them. ''The Coming Race,'' for example, depicts the sixth race that is now being born in America; and his other mystic novels, such as ''The Strange Story,'' ''Haunted House,'' and that great Occult novel, ''Zanoni,'' all reveal much to those who are interested in Occultism. The novel, ''Zanoni,'' is really the story of one-half of a soul trying to find its other half, and it portrays the dangers of different kinds that beset the student on his evolutionary journey. Zanoni finds the woman—the other half of his soul—but she is engaged to marry a person who is anxious to study Occultism. Zanoni seeks an old Occultist, who agrees to accept the young man as a student, providing he gives up his lady love to Zanoni. The youth has pursued his studies but a short time when he comes in contact with the ''dwellers upon the threshold,'' which in the novel are depicted as being tremendous forces and entities that were turned loose upon the defenceless boy. We read

how all the sediment of his nature was brought
out, how he was tempted, and how he yielded to
temptation, and at last went to moral destruction.

These "dwellers on the threshold" are what we
all have to face when we contact the psychic realm,
and not only do the students of Occultism have to
meet them, but the whole human race, as it develops, must come in contact with this realm. So
let us see who and what these "dwellers on the
threshold" are. Many of them are detached objective minds. We have seen in another lecture
how the objective and subjective minds were
united and became men. We also saw that a battle
has to be waged between these two minds when
the subjective awakens, and undertakes the control
of its affairs. In the course of time the fight between these two minds of man becomes so tremendous that there sometimes comes a cleavage
between the two, and the subjective conquers its
lower mind, making of it a tractable vehicle. But
sometimes the objective mind is stronger than the
subjective, and refuses to be governed. Then it is
that a separation comes, and the objective mind,
strong in its victory, becomes detached from its
subjective. The subjective, being unwilling to
remain under the dominion of its objective mind,
leaves it to its ultimate destruction, and goes back
into the Infinite, to rest until another Cosmic Day

shall come, when it can start forth with a new objective mind.

This rebellious objective mind is so strong that it may continue to occupy its physical body for several years after the separation, and goes through the remainder of that life the semblance of a human being, but devoid of moral character. When it excarnates and its body is destroyed, it may or may not be strong enough to reincarnate. If it does, then it will be of an intellectual animal nature, with no conception of morality or spirituality. In case it is not strong enough to reincarnate, it becomes a "dweller upon the threshold," an individualized consciousness upon the subjective side of life, invisible to the physical eyes of men, but active in its destructive desires and purposes. It becomes one of the many unpleasant forces or entities which we have to come in contact with when we reach the psychic realm.

In your study of mankind you will find many of these objective minds without their subjective or higher principle, and this is especially true among the older races and sub-races. We find them here in our own country, but not in such large numbers as in China, Japan, and in Egypt. These are the persons whom we are pleased to designate as degenerates and perverts, also many of our most hardened criminals. Such entities seem to be maliciously wicked, and persistently destroy and pull down everyone with whom they associate. These are they who excarnate and go to the first plane of the subjective world and become the dwellers upon the threshold.

But there are other denizens of that plane. Every soul that excarnates, if it is not able to pass into the planes beyond, by reason of its undevelopment and strong animal nature, must remain there, and become a dweller on the threshold also. Then there is the third class of dwellers called elementals. These centers of consciousness and force have not developed to the point where incarnation is possible for them. They are the fairies, goblins, brownies and undines. These entities are not fanciful creations of the imagination, as many persons suppose, for they do exist in elemental forms; and when they have been seen and described by persons whose psychic sense made them conscious of them, they were realities. Man cannot imagine that which does not exist, for no one can make a picture of the non-existent.

Elementals are created by the thoughts of men. As man develops he thinks more and more forcefully; and as he thinks, he creates little centers of consciousness within Divine Mind. These centers of consciousness assume different forms according to the quality of the thoughts which created them. The elemental grows very much in the same manner that the embryo grows while living off its mother. These centers which man creates draw strength and vitality from him, and remain within the photosphere of their creator. But since whatever is created upon the mental plane must, in course of time, objectivize, or embody itself in a physical form, some time these elementals must take on material bodies of some kind. There are the so-called good and bad elementals and when they become embodied in animal or insect form, that form will be assumed which corresponds to the nature of the consciousness seeking embodiment. If the elemental be of a mischievous, destructive nature, then it was the result of mischievous, destructive thoughts of man, and will take upon itself the form of animal or insect that will annoy man and destroy his property. Because it is a law that whatsoever man sends forth mentally must and will return to him.

Then there is still another kind of thought creations of men which become embodied soon after they are born. These are the licentious, obscene thoughts of both sexes, that become the creeping, crawling bugs and vermin which infest untidy homes, second- and third-class hotels and public houses. Then there are the biting, stinging thoughts which embody themselves as flies, wasps, bees and mosquitoes; and the poisonous thoughts which become spiders and reptiles. These miserable creatures, born of man's lower mind, cannot use the atoms of a higher rate of vibration for their bodies, but must use those atoms with which they vibrate harmoniously. They gather up the diseased atoms, the dirty atoms, those atoms which can no longer be used by men or beasts, and through forms composed of these, express themselves upon the material plane. And thus man himself creates the destructive things of earth which turn and wage war against him; for "God saw everything that He had made, and behold it was very good."

When an entity has attained a sufficient density within the subjective realm to be ready for embodiment, it has come to a point where it can have a direct influence upon human life, and it then reacts upon its creator according to the nature that was given it. When these elementals separate from the photosphere in which they were created, they often leave their creator, and impinge upon the auras of other persons. Sometimes they are utilized in magic, particularly in that form known as ceremonial magic, and students of Occultism sometimes use them for the purpose of producing psychic phenomena. The transference of material substances from one room to another through closed doors and solid walls, or the disintegration and reintegration of so-called solid things are performed through utilizing these elemental forces of nature.

Then there are the minds of animals, or animal souls, if you choose to so designate those centers of consciousness, which have been embodied, have excarnated and have passed on to the subjective side of nature to await another opportunity to become re-embodied. These subjective entities still possess all their animal propensities, but have no physical means of expressing them and they belong to the vast multitude of dwellers upon the threshold.

Where is this threshold? In Catholicism it is known as Purgatory; in Protestantism it is Hades. You remember the words of the Creed: "He descended into Hades." Hades is the place for departed spirits. It is the sidereal realm of the medieval mystic; it is the astral or psychic plane of the modern mystic and theosophist; it is the first plane of the spiritualist, the plane for earth-bound souls. It is here interpenetrating this physical world of ours. We have seen in another lecture that this earth is surrounded by five belts or zones which extend out into space, according to their color and vibration. This threshold is the first of the subjective planes, and is called the threshold because it is the crossing over point from objective life into subjective life, and is the doorway through which egos re-enter earth life. All souls must pass through it, but the higher developed ones stay there but a very short time and never a moment after they are liberated from their physical bodies. This is one of the reasons why Occultists advocate cremation of the physical body, because by this process the man in a few moments is free to go to the plane where he belongs instead of being chained to his body on the threshold for weeks, months, or years, as the case may be. Souls are magnetically bound to their bodies, and until "the silver cord is loosened" they cannot be free. Catholics say masses for the souls of the dead that these souls may be released from the threshold, or purgatory. Years ago, when many of the priests were Occultists, a mass was written or chanted in the musical key which corresponded to the color of the deceased. The sound of the chanted mass disrupted the "silver cord," as a prolonged sound upon the physical plane will disrupt a material mass, if its keynote be sounded long enough.

As man's vibrations are raised he necessarily contacts with this first subjective realm; and the influence of the four classes of entities, previously mentioned and popularly known as the psychic forces of nature, are exerted upon him. The unconscious sensitive is always susceptible to influences which produce moods that other persons do not have. At times he feels great depression, fears impending calamities and is influenced in various ways by the denizens of the next plane.

And when an excarnated objective mind who has lost its higher mind finds a sensitive person whom it can control in mind and body, it immediately commences to manage his affairs. It enjoys by proxy, as it were, the intoxicating liquors that it forces its victim to drink. It gratifies its lusts by controlling its victim, and compelling him to sin. It revenges itself, through its ignorant victim, upon persons whom it hates. Fearful crimes are many times committed by persons who are almost or quite unconscious of what they are doing, and who waken to consciousness inside prison walls to be told of their terrible deeds. In cases of emotional insanity, where a man temporarily loses self-control and murders another, could the matter be investigated from the psychic side of life, it would be seen that the murderer was often but an unconscious victim of a disembodied fiend, who desired to commit the murder, and used the unfortunate sensitive as an instrument.

The denizens of the next plane, and especially the excarnated minds of depraved men and women and the detached objective minds, utilize mankind for the purpose of vicarious enjoyment. A drunkard does not lose his love for liquor when he leaves his physical body. There is nothing in the process of the change called death which changes character. "In the place where the tree falleth, there it shall be." It is natural that a drunkard should wish to enjoy what he considers the pleasure of drinking, and so he selects a subject that he can influence. This sensitive, whose will is not strong enough to resist this strange influence which is thrown upon him, yields to the temptation, and is overpowered. He indulges what he believes to be his own appetite for rum and the more he drinks the more he wants. When he is overcome with the fumes of liquor he is crowded out of his body by the controlling entity, who takes possession of it, and enjoys a vicarious drunk at the expense of his sensitive victim. A love for gambling, intense sex desire, civic wrongs and all kinds of crime are often traceable for their cause to what many persons call at this time "spirit control." When we read of a horrible murder or crime being committed by some man who declares "God spoke" and told him to do it, you may know the cause was just behind the scenes, and the crime was instigated by a dweller on the threshold.

There are semi-conscious sensitives who are influenced by the denizens of the next plane. By semi-conscious sensitives I mean persons who have reached a point in their development where they are conscious of the existence of a psychic plane, but do not know the nature of it. They are conscious of psychic forces, but do not know the nature of those forces. Most persons, when they reach this point in their development, begin to investigate psychic phenomena immediately. A student of Occultism who is a conscious sensitive, is required to develop upon the mental plane before he is permitted to study the psychic realm. He must first attain the proper poise and development by learning to think clearly. Then he is taught how to use Cosmic Forces, and to surround himself with protecting currents, before he is taught how to function upon the psychic plane. After this has been accomplished he can look down upon the psychic realm and can penetrate into it without fear of attracting to himself unpleasant companions, or getting into unfortunate or compromising situations.

It is impossible for ignorant or semi-ignorant persons to investigate the psychic realm without being more or less influenced by it, and perhaps it will be well for us to examine the various classes of investigators, and see something of the dangers to which they are subjected. I think we may safely group the investigators of spiritualistic phenomena or spiritualism in the first class, and this class should also include the members of the Society for Psychical Research, and kindred organizations, because these are nothing more nor less than investigators of Spiritualism under the guise of science. Spiritualism is necromancy revamped, and is a practice that has been inveighed against by those who knew the dangers attending it, and by those who wrote the sacred books, since mankind came upon this earth. Its six chief aspects are automatic writing, inspirational writing, inspirational speaking, trance mediumship, independent slate writing, and materializing mediumship. In all of these, passivity is the sine qua non of success, because mediumship is the end in view, and passivity is the means by which it is to be attained.

And after mediumship is attained, what does it mean? Simply that this person has become an instrument through whom these excarnated, unattached objective minds and other denizens of the psychic plane, may speak or write, or perform like clowns in a circus. And what good comes from it? These entities, many of them, have become detached from their own higher principle, and must live on someone in order that their existence may be prolonged. Because without its subjective, the objective mind slowly deteriorates, and after a time fades out. These ignorant or malicious lower minds personate our departed friends, and glibly give us instructions about our domestic and business matters. They advise us when and where to buy and sell stocks; they give us long lectures on religion, and advise us about the training of our children. Think of such a creature as Jack the Ripper giving us a lecture on morality! Sometimes these "angel guides"—for so they insist upon being called—aspire to fame, and pose as Lincoln, Shakespeare, or Napoleon, forgetting that at that moment, at a dozen places in different cities of the world, alleged Lincolns, Shakespeares and Napoleons are doing the same thing. They urge us to become mediums and organize developing circles in order that they may teach us political reforms or all about the eternal progression of the soul. And all the time we are studying under them and are worshiping at their séances, they are absorbing our magnetism and are ruining, mentally, morally, physically, and often financially, those persons who become their mediums. For mediumship soon becomes either possession or obsession, and both these conditions lead to insanity. In discussing this question hereafter, the term obsession will be used to designate all classes of cases where a human body is wholly or in part controlled by a disembodied entity.

Most of the insanity of the present day is due to obsession; and insanity increases as humanity becomes more sensitive to the influence of these dwellers upon the threshold. There are cases of hallucination when an insane person believes he has exchanged his personality for that of another; or who fancies he is a distinguished personage, and insists upon being treated with great homage. Epilepsy is nearly always attributable to obsession, and the best treatment for all these cases is mental treatment. Making the patient positive will restore self-control and health where medicine and confinement will utterly fail.

An investigator of the psychic plane, of the first class, must either become a medium himself, or use a medium for the purpose of studying that plane. In either case he is subjected to imposition relative to the cause of the phenomena obtained. It is a well-known fact that a large percentage of the communications received from so-called spirits are untrue, or are of a nature one would not expect from the inhabitants of that plane. Mediumship usually leads eventually to insanity or to the premature death of the medium. Even when there seems to be a controlling entity of a comparatively higher order than is usually found on that plane, there is necessarily a constant diminution of the medium's forces. And as the vital force of the medium diminishes, he becomes unreliable, and frequently has to resort to fraud and pretence in order to continue his exhibitions. Everyone who knows anything about this subject cannot deny that there are sometimes genuine phenomena, but more often they are simulated. But one result can come from such fraudulent practices, and that is degeneracy of the moral character of the medium and of all who associate with him in his dishonorable business. Many mediums become habitual drunkards as a consequence of having to take intoxicating liquor to stimulate their failing strength after being vampirized into a weakened condition by the entities that control them and absorb their magnetism.

It is admitted by unprejudiced investigators of psychism that the majority of "Spirit Controls" are of a "low order." But this is explained by their statement that "like attracts like," and that mediums and investigators attract "spirits" of a nature kindred to themselves. It is also admitted by all investigators that a positive, strong character is incapable of becoming a medium, and frequently prevents phenomena from taking place at a séance when he is present. Taking these two statements into consideration, it is logical to conclude that there are no positive, strong characters who attempt to control men, as the Occultists who have a knowledge of the subjective planes of being have always maintained.

And after all, what has been gained from all the phenomena from any one of the five sources mentioned? Has any new philosophy been presented, or any great discovery been made, through these "spirit guides"? "By their fruits ye shall know them," and the result of the investigations of the Society for Psychical Research along these lines have merely verified the phenomena given by the Spiritualists since 1849, and not one of the investigators has as yet discovered the true cause of the phenomena, or formulated the law under which they occur. One of the greatest tests given by these mediums is this. Some entity speaks or writes through them to someone concerning matters that were known only to the departed and to the investigator. But this is no proof that the controlling entity is the soul of the dear departed, because any disembodied entity can read the mind of the investigator, and can see the thought pictures that are in his aura. In this manner the past of any person may be read, because it is written around him in his photosphere, and goes with him wherever he goes.

A local preacher says he receives communications from his dead son and cites facts only known to himself and that son. These communications he declares are proofs of the identity of his deceased son. He says his son revealed to him where certain articles and papers were after he, the son, had passed from this life, and that he himself did not even know of the existence of them. This is no proof that the information came from the man's son, because any disembodied entity could have done the same; and it is just as likely that the information was given by the objective mind of Captain Kidd as it is that it came from the preacher's son.

The second class of investigators may be known

as passive clairvoyants, or those persons who cultivate passive mediumship for the purpose of functioning upon the subjective plane. Such a clairvoyant permits an entity to enfold or envelop his body while it impresses a mental picture upon his mind and then the medium describes the picture he sees. This is not true clairvoyance, because the entity that impresses the medium is responsible for the picture, and it may be nothing but a fanciful creation of its own. The medium has not seen a reality, but has looked at the mental creations of another; and when we consider the character of most controlling entities, we feel safe in saying that possibly their pictures may not be altogether reliable.

The third class of investigators may be called artificial clairvoyants and is composed largely of crystal gazers, magic-mirror gazers, etc., who, by these practices, throw themselves into a self-induced semi-hypnosis. In this state or condition they become susceptible to psychical influences, and mentally impressed pictures are the result. Vanity, or the desire for money-making, is usually the cause for this kind of practice, rather than a desire for growth or development, and the dangers from psychic influences are fully as great as in the classes before mentioned.

But there is a true clairvoyance or seership which depends upon two things—a well-developed subjective mind that rules its objective mind, and a peculiar physiological condition. Nearly in the center of the brain of every human being is situated a tiny organ called the pineal gland, and this is the chief center through which the mind must function, in order that man may possess the X-ray vision that enables him to look beyond the material plane, upon the inner or subjective planes of consciousness. This gland can be attuned to finer vibrations than register in any of our other senses, and these vibrations relate us to the inner worlds or planes. The student of Occultism, at a certain point in his progress, is taught how to direct special cosmic currents of force into this gland to enlarge and raise its vibrations. When this has been accomplished, the student can function upon the subjective plane by an effort of his will as easily and well as he can see on the objective plane by opening his physical eyes. With this class of clairvoyants there is no passivity or trance condition, but there is a conscious shifting of the consciousness from one plane to another; and it is according to the development of the man whether or not he is able to function upon many or few of the subjective planes of being.

The unattached student of Occultism is one without a Master or Teacher. He is one who knows of Occult powers and forces, and longs to possess them, and he courageously faces the dangers without assistance. This great desire for growth leads him to seek quick development, which is natural. The great majority of people, when they first hear of Occultism, and Occult teachers, immediately want a teacher, and their cry goes up: "Give us a teacher." Then they begin to think they are developing rapidly in Occultism and when certain subjective influences come about and they feel their peculiar vibrations, they immediately conclude that a Master has come to teach and help them. These subjective entities, wishing to gain control of ambitious students, impress them with the thought they love to entertain, and soon these students of Occultism are under the influence, and perhaps under the absolute control of the dwellers upon the threshold.

Let me tell you now and let it always remain with you, that *no teacher of Occultism will ever try to control you in mind or body. You are divine because you are a part of Deity and therefore your body and your life are yours. A teacher has no more right to control your mind than he has to violate your body and no student, teacher, or Master of Occultism will ever attempt it.* So when you feel peculiar influences around you, or if you hear voices saying, "We have come to help you, you are progressing rapidly," you may know it is the dwellers on the threshold who are talking to you. All students of Occultism, whether at-

tached or unattached, are helped by the Great
Ones, but only when they are earnestly trying
to help themselves. *They are never touched or
coerced, or worked upon subjectively.*

If you are trying to work out a problem, you
may suddenly receive an idea which will make
everything plain to you. If you are ill, you may
suddenly receive a suggestion to go somewhere, or
do something which will help you to recover your
health. If you are out of a position and need
money, something or someone may be brought forward to help you. The student who is studying
along these deeper lines is always watched and
will be helped when he deserves help. The student who declares that he is going to work out his
own salvation, that he is going to develop, and
uses the knowledge he has gained to live according
to his ideal, is a probationer, and if he persists
in this course for a period of seven years he will
draw to himself a teacher in physical form. That
teacher may be a Master, an Adept, or an advanced student, but a teacher who is best suited
to him in his development at that time. And during the seven years of probation, help will be
given to him in various ways.

It does not follow that everyone who thinks he
is ready for the higher Occult teachings is really
prepared for them. For example, during the last
century a number of persons heard of the Mas-

ters and Adepts, and seventy-two curious individuals started out to become students. An Adept whom I know promised to give them one year of probation on the condition that those who successfully stood all the tests given during that year should be accepted students. The first thing he did was to tell each aspirant after Occult teachings what kind of life he had lived, and was living at that time. He told them about their faults, and how those faults should be corrected. He took away their wines and all kinds of intoxicating liquors and also their pipes and tobacco; he forbade gambling and immoral associates and ordered certain hours set apart for meditation and concentration. In less than one week one-half the number of aspirants for Occult knowledge turned their backs on Occultism in indignation. The others struggled on for a while, but were so badly beset by their old habits and by the subjective entities that were aroused by the new order of things and who immediately set about trying to drag these students back into their old habits of living, that one after another fell out of line, till at the end of the year only one person out of the seventy-two had succeeded in living up to his promises. This man was given permission to withdraw from the world and go into a lodge, where he was taught Occultism.

Let those who desire to push on in their evolution take the attitude that they will not study psychic forces at all; that they will not look for a Master in that realm of being; that they will begin work by building up character and by practicing what has been taught; for I tell you truly, the psychic realm can offer you absolutely nothing of value at this time.   It is the higher and better knowledge that you can utilize, that you should desire; the true Occultism which teaches the laws of being.

LECTURE NINE

HYPNOTISM, AND HOW TO GUARD AGAINST IT

IN 1734 an old student of Occultism re-incarnated. His life was not dissimilar from the life of his associates except that he had the benefit of a better early education, and an opportunity to study medicine later on in his life. He attended a medical college in Vienna and graduated in 1766, and soon after that time resumed his study of Occultism under the same Master who had taught him in the previous life. It required but a very short time, after he began the practice of medicine, for him to learn something about the deficiencies in the system of therapeutics, as it was then understood. In 1778 he moved to Paris, which was then the scientific world, and began the practice of a system of magnetic treatments of the sick which startled the scientists and brought down upon him the condemnation of many of the medical men of that time. He cured many cases that the physicians had pronounced incurable and, of course, aroused the jealousy and hatred of many of the medical profession. I am speaking of Friedrich Anton Mesmer.

The cures this man performed were so very remarkable that all the wealth and intelligence of the world went to Paris to be treated by this new system, and as a result, the medical profession began to wage war against him as they did during this last century against the Christian and Mental Scientists and the Osteopaths. For human nature was then no better than now, and the green-eyed monster of jealousy cut a very conspicuous figure with the treatment of Mesmer, as it does with all other persons who innovate old methods. After Mesmer's fame became unbearable to the scientists, an investigating committee was appointed to look into the new system. It reported adversely to Mesmer, of course, and soon his clientèle began falling away from him.

In 1783 he founded the Order of Universal Harmony, a secret order built upon the lines of Occultism, under the direction of his teacher, who was also in Paris, giving many great demonstrations of his Occult powers. I refer to Count Saint-Germain. This Order of Universal Harmony was the gateway through which all persons could enter, who were prepared at that time to take up Occult studies. But as time passed, many of the members dropped out and the Order gradually grew smaller and smaller until but a very few were left. To these faithful ones Mesmer taught the Occult system of therapeutics, Occultism, and the manipulation of that force which he designated as Mesmerism—naming it modestly after himself. After the public had deserted him, and most of his students had turned their attention to other things than Occultism, he removed to England, where he met with very little success, and finally went back to the Fatherland, where it is said he died in 1815.

After that date, for many years nothing was heard from his students, or from his system; but in 1841 Doctor Braid, of Manchester, England, commenced to investigate along Mesmer's lines of thought, and inaugurated a system somewhat similar in principle, which he called Braidism, but which subsequently became known as hypnotism. Later, some scientific students in Paris and elsewhere began investigating along the lines laid down by Dr. Braid, and just about a century after Mesmer had been condemned and called an impostor by the French scientists, his teachings began to receive the attention they deserved, although many persons, while accepting the teachings, discredited the teacher.

There was a difference, however, between Mesmer's and Braid's systems. Mesmer taught that mesmerism is an emanation of certain particles called animal magnetism, from one person which affects the will and nervous system of another. Braid taught that there is no emanation from the operator, but either through the will of the operator, or through mechanical processes, an artificial mental condition is awakened in the subject, and that during this condition the volition of the subject is under the control of the operator. In other words, it is the influence of one mind over another. How one mind can affect another without an emanation is beyond the comprehension of the lecturer, but perhaps hypnotists can explain that condition satisfactorily, at least to themselves. These are the supposed lines of division between the two systems, but Mesmer really taught two systems in one. First, that there is a flow of magnetic force, which he designated as animal magnetism, and that this emanating force is curative in its nature; second, that there can be coercion of mind by mind. He practiced the first and warned his students against practicing the other. The world, of course, confused his teachings, as it usually confuses anything of an Occult nature, and remembered the second system without his caution.

At the present time animal magnetism is known as Mesmerism, and Hypnotism is known as sleep, artificially produced. So we shall try to follow out the modern conception of it rather than the presentation of Mesmer, although reference may be had from time to time to Mesmer's teachings. He taught that Mesmerism is a Cosmic Force which is a part of the law of love or the law of attraction, and that it flows through man and may be directed

by his will, as an emanation from him to another.
For example, he showed that the force flowing
from his hands was a force that he could draw
into himself and then give to another. He also
showed that he could get approximately the same
effect by using large magnets, thus proving that
this is a general and not a personal force which
he used.

The law of gravitation is a part of this magnetic force, and so is love in all its gradations,
whether it be human love, animal love, or passion.
The law of attraction manifesting through an animal body we now designate as animal magnetism.
This Cosmic Force, passing through an animal, is
nothing more nor less than the Universal Life
Principle, the orange vibration, which you will be
taught in the next lecture how to use. Passing
through man as human-animal magnetism, it
manifests itself as that peculiar vibration or
force which his development permits.

There is, however, a physiological condition
necessary to a body in order to make it magnetic,
just as there is a physical condition necessary to
make any mass magnetic. For example: Glass is
not magnetic as compared with iron or steel. The
rate of vibration of glass is so different from that
of magnetism that it does not make a good con-
ductor for that force as it flows over it. The condition necessary to make a proper basis for the

animal or human magnetism to manifest is the excess, above the normal, of the number of red blood corpuscles in the body; and these red corpuscles must vibrate at a high rate. With these two conditions there is established the physiological basis which enables the Cosmic Force to manifest; and having the proper physiological basis, a person, either consciously or unconsciously, draws within himself this Cosmic Force through the left side of his body, and passes it out through his right side, the left being the negative, and the right the positive side of the body.

Animal magnetism can be utilized by man through the blending of his aura with that of another, or through transmission by physical contact, laying on of the hands, etc. Most persons, such as faith curers, or magnetic healers, use this magnetic force without an understanding of the law which underlies it. If an Occultist desires to transmit this force to another person by physical means, he places his right hand on that other person; then, after drawing into himself the force, he permits it to flow through him into the other. This force can be used advantageously in all nervous troubles, because it is the nerve fluid, or life force, which restores depletion; it is also helpful in cases of consumption of any of the physical organs of the body, and if properly directed, will build up diseased cells and restore wasted tissues. Many persons possess this magnetic force to a great degree, but do not know how to use it, while others perform cures unconscious of the power they possess, and without the action of their own will.

A person who makes a practice of using his animal magnetism or life force for the treating of disease must become greatly depleted at times, since the natural inflow of life force is never so great as the outflow. If the natural inflow of the life force were throughout life as great as the outflow, our bodies would last forever, because this would make an even exchange of atoms, and no robbery could be perpetrated. There is an actual emanation from one person to another, and this emanation causes an exchange of physical atoms. Remember, please, that I am not speaking of the higher Cosmic forces which can be used for healing purposes without depleting the healer, and which I shall teach you how to use in a subsequent lecture; but I am speaking of the natural life force within the physical body, that can be used as a curative agency, as Mesmer used it.

It is because of the outflow exceeding the inflow of magnetism that many drugless healers suffer so much depletion after their professional manipulations—which are very good for the patients, but hard for them. Sometimes the drugless healer absorbs the old diseased atoms from his patients, through manipulating with both hands at the same time, thus forming a complete circuit for the magnetic force, which carries from him his best atoms and returns the cast-off ones from his patients. It is not conducive to the good health of the drugless or magnetic healer, to use both hands while treating the sick; but in severe cases, where it seems that a life should be kept from going out, it may be done. But immediately afterward both hands and arms should be bathed in hot water, rubbing the arms and hands from the elbow downward to the tips of the fingers. In this way it is possible to remove, by aid of the hot water, many of the low vibrating atoms which have been taken into the system.

When a Mental Healer begins to lose his force, or power to heal, as many do, the world says: "If Mind is infinite, why has this healer failed?" The reason is this: First, his brain has become tired by continuous concentration, and its material atoms have taken a slower rate of vibration because the outflow of magnetic force has been much greater than the inflow. Through his intense interest in his cases perhaps his sympathies have gone out to his patients with his treatments, and there was an expenditure of emotional force. Without understanding the reason for his waning power, he tries to go on with the work of healing when he should rest and sleep, and in this manner draw back to himself the life force he has given away. After a time he finds himself depleted and is compelled to retire from service humiliated and chagrined, perhaps, because of the unkind criticisms he has received from those to whom he has given his life force.

There is a better and a higher way to treat the sick than by the magnetic force which made Mesmer famous, and that is to remain in a positive condition of mind, control your sympathies, and thus hold your own magnetic force as a basis over which you may draw the higher Cosmic forces, and pass them on to your patients without so greatly depleting yourself. If you can control your sympathies, and remain positive, you can treat without serious depletion as many patients as you can entertain during office hours. *If you cannot remain positive it is then better to direct mentally the Cosmic Forces without physical contact with the patient.* But, you may say, this is not the aspect that modern science is investigating. It is true that it is not practiced along the lines Mesmer laid down, except by the physicians who are beginning to use electricity in their practice, and who attempt to do with their batteries precisely what Mesmer attempted to do with his magnets; and I am not sure that they are any more successful, because Mesmer also used the greater force of mind to assist these currents.

And now we come to that particular aspect of

the subject which modern science is beginning to
investigate, which is known as hypnotism. Hypnotism is artificial sleep, which may be produced
upon one's self or upon another; and it may be
produced by the power of will, by mechanical processes, or by the will supplemented by mechanical
processes. The mechanisms that are used to produce hypnosis are revolving mirrors, bright lights,
or anything which will serve to excite the optic
nerves and raise them to a rate of vibration which
will enable the subject to pass into hypnosis, or
sleep. Unnatural stimulation of the nerves of the
eyes, or of the nerves at the base of the brain, or
by focusing the sight at an angle of forty-five
degrees, and then gradually raising it until the
pupils are turned upward above the upper lids,
will produce an abnormal nervous excitation; and
while the subject is in this condition he readily
accepts the mental suggestion of sleep, and passes
into hypnosis. In this manner he is forced out of
his physical body, is under the control of the
operator's mind, and is also exposed to any or all
influences upon the subjective plane which he has
abnormally invaded. If the hypnosis is complete,
then both minds of the subject are absolutely
under the control of the operator; but if the hypnosis be only partial, then nothing but the objective, or lower mind, of the subject is controlled.
But while in this condition, and passive to the will

of another, the subject must accept as true everything suggested to him by that controlling mind;
and whatever command is given to him in sleep
he will obey when he wakes, and without knowing
why. From the first moment the subject yields
his will to another he becomes that other's slave,
if that one desires to make him so. So long as the
operator lives in this world, so long will he be
able to control that subject, unless his power
is broken.

It is contended by the modern hypnotist in
France and in America that the mind of the subject is not dominated to the extent of coercion, or
beyond the power of the subject to act independently. In other words, that he cannot be compelled
to do a wrong against his will. Cases are cited
where subjects refused to stab a man when the
operators gave them real daggers and commanded
them to do so. Other cases are cited where the
same subjects were given paper daggers and
were told to strike designated persons. This command they obeyed with alacrity; and because they
obeyed in the last instances and refused in the
first, it was supposed that they could not be coerced to commit a crime against their wills. The
Occultists say these cases do not prove the theory
advanced, but only show that both minds of the
subjects were not under the control of the operator; and that if they were, the subjects would

have obeyed in the first instances as quickly as in the last. Then too there were in the former cases mental reservations in one or both minds of the operators which affected the subject. Occultists who have made a study of the power of mind for hundreds of years, say that nothing will prevent a hypnotized subject from obeying the commands of the operator, or controlling mind, when once the subject is fully under his influence.

Some of you may have seen the account in one of our local papers where a man was hypnotized and compelled to deed everything he had in the world to another man. After the victim became conscious of what he had done, he appealed to his attorney, who took the matter into court, but when the victim appeared to testify, the hypnotist would not permit him to speak and the man's throat was paralyzed in the presence of the room full of people. The hypnotist was incarcerated in jail until the paralysis passed away from the throat of his victim and when his influence was removed and the true testimony was given, the court decided that the property should be restored to the original owner. And only a few months ago here in New York City, you remember how Patrick was tried and convicted of the murder of the millionaire Rice. It was proved that it was the old man's valet who had killed him while under the hypnotic influence of Patrick; and these are only two cases that have come to the public's notice. It is gradually being understood, however, that morality does not enter at all into the question of control, but that it depends wholly upon whether or not both minds of the subject are controlled. Occultists believe that there is no disease, no trouble, nor anything in the world that can justify a person in attempting to hypnotize another. If a person consents to be hypnotized, then it is because he does not know the dangers he incurs by consenting, and his ignorance should not be taken advantage of by one who knows better.

There is another phase of this mind controlling mind which is more subtle and dangerous than that of mechanical hypnotism, because it can be used without the knowledge of the subject, and without the immediate presence of the operator. This branch is called by the Occultists Mental Dominion, and is just beginning to be understood in the West. Hypnotism by mental dominion is produced by mental suggestion alone, without physical contact or mechanical aids. It makes no difference whether the subject be present, in the next room, or in the same State with the operator, he can be reached equally well at any time or place. The method formerly adopted was to suggest sleep to the subject, or victim, and when he had received and obeyed the suggestion, then the operator impressed whatever he desired upon the mind of his subject, who had to obey his will upon waking. But after a time the American Hypnotists discovered that putting the subject to sleep was not essential, and that just as effective work could be done by repeated suggestion until the subject should accept and act upon it, believing it to be his own thought. This process of mental control can only be called hypnotism by courtesy, since hypnosis is now omitted as a necessary condition in its accomplishment; however, it will continue to be called by that name until a more suitable one shall be adopted.

Unless you have made a study of this practice of mental dominion, you have no idea of the extent to which this subtle power is being used in the United States. It is flagrantly and openly taught by "colleges," chartered by various States; all newspapers, and many magazines, contain their alluring advertisements offering to teach "Personal Magnetism," "Hypnotism," "The Secret of Power," etc., etc. Under various names each of these teachers, colleges, professors, and doctors offers for a monetary consideration to teach you how to dominate your fellow men, how to enslave another Son of God, and how to *"positively enable any intelligent person to exercise a marvelous influence over anyone whom he may wish to control."* I quote from one of the largest and most persistent advertisers of this branch of education.

Traveling salesmen, doctors, lawyers, brokers, real estate men, and, in fact, persons in every branch of business are studying and using mental coercion.

In my own personal experience, in the practice of law, I have had a dozen or more cases in which the malign influence of persons had been used to get money and property away from others. In three of these cases stock brokers had used mental coercion compelling my clients to entrust money to their keeping with the permission to use it as the broker saw fit. The money had been appropriated by the hypnotist stock broker for his own purposes, and my demand for restitution was met with the assertion that it had been lost in speculation by my client. In two of these cases, after the arrest of the respective brokers, the proceedings had to be stopped, because my clients had again yielded to the influence of the men who had coerced them and refused to prosecute them further.

There is a member of this class who heard these lectures last year and said that such an influence could never come into her life; yet within a few months afterward, while her husband was away and she was alone, a stock broker called, and asked her to place in his hands a large block of valuable stock with full permission to dispose of it as he thought best. After urging the matter for an unreasonable length of time, he finally left her, after gaining her promise to let him call the next day for the stock. After he had gone the woman began to realize that the man had influenced her against her will and judgment and she wrote to him refusing to see him or to let him have the stock. Then for three days she had to fight his mental suggestions to change her mind and accept his offer, but finally succeeded in saving her property.

Another member of my class, who heard this lecture last year, thought she was exempt from such influences because of the quiet, retired life she was living. She discovered her mistake when a stranger called one day and persuaded her to give him a large contract for advertising a book she had written. After securing this he called again in a few days, and tried to coerce her into giving to him her rights and copyright to the book; and had it not been for the sudden recollection of what she had heard about hypnotism and also for the aid of another member of her family, who was a student along this line, the hypnotist would have succeeded in getting what he wanted. As it was, he very nearly put her to sleep and she had a hard battle to resist complete hypnosis.

When the Countess Wachmeister was in this country, several years ago, she told of the following case: There were three men in this city who had studied hypnotism and decided to combine their efforts and victimize a wealthy man. They each took a turn in working upon him mentally during each day, sending suggestion after suggestion to him, until he became absolutely under the influence of the trio. After a time he became so sensitive that the picture of the face of each of his tormentors would rise before his mental vision while he was being worked upon. Then he could hear them speak to each other, but continued to resist them until he went to sleep from weariness. But when he awoke he was impelled to write a check and send it to the address that had been impressed upon his mind. This kind of robbery continued for some time and finally the victim went to the Countess, and asked her to deliver him from the power of his tormentors.

There is no limit to the power of mind, nor to its field of operation through suggestion. In the beginning of the use of Occult forces, suggestion is one of the most powerful of the mind's instruments which the student learns to use. It should not be identified with hypnotism although it can be used to produce hypnosis. Like any other force, it can be used for good or for evil, and the line that lies between the right and wrong use of it is as narrow as the edge of a knife, and is just as sharp. In the practice of magic these two ways diverge, and we find what is called White and Black Magic. The first is a straight and narrow path which leads to the mountain top of power and wisdom, and to.

reach it is salvation. The other is the broad road which leads to pitfalls and destruction; and I regret to say that many souls are enticed to travel therein. It was the wrong use of this power of suggestion which destroyed us as Atlanteans, and from the present indications it would seem that we did not learn, through that sad experience, that we have no right to enslave the minds of others.

Mind must be reached by thought, if the thought be constantly repeated, and nothing can prevent a suggestion from reaching its destination, because telepathy is based upon law. But whether the suggestion shall be accepted and acted upon depends upon the recipient to decide; and it is upon the acceptance or rejection of suggestion that the freedom or enslavement of a mind is determined. There are different kinds of suggestion, two of which are known as audible and silent. Audible suggestion we are constantly indulging in, and is something we should learn to control, because it may be either constructive or destructive, and if the latter, we may do much harm to others. For example: We meet a friend who looks tired, and we say: "How bad you look; are you ill?" This is a destructive suggestion, and may have the effect of really making our friend ill if he accepts it as a truth. Parents and teachers are constantly making audible suggestions to children which have a great effect upon them. If a teacher calls his pupils dunces and dolts, and tells them how stupid they are, he is pretty sure to find in them just what he suggests. If a parent tells his child that if he misses his lesson he will be punished, that child will remember the suggestion of punishment and probably miss his lesson, because the suggestion of punishment brings an element of fear with it which makes an indelible impression upon the child's mind. It is a destructive suggestion, because it destroys the child's ability to learn his lesson. But if the parent were to say "You can learn your lesson, because you are a bright, intelligent child," the suggestion would be constructive, and the child would respond to it by having a desire awakened in him to learn, since the mind of a child is plastic, and is easily impressed by audible suggestion.

The objective mind is always ready to see the dark side of life, and will readily accept any audible suggestion of a destructive nature; and since there are constructive suggestions which can be made to help others, why should we be continually hindering instead of helping our friends? Why is it not better to bring sunshine rather than shadows into their lives? Suppose a friend of yours is about to make a business connection with a Mr. Jones, whom you slightly know, and you say, for the sake of gossip, "Mr. Jones is a dishonest man." This suggestion, whether true or untrue,

will have a tendency to make Mr. Jones dishonest
if he hears of what you have said, because the
thought dishonesty has been impressed upon his
mind, and he will think he may as well be what
people think he is. Then your friend to whom
you made the suggestion will think of it when he
sees Mr. Jones, and the unfortunate man will get
both silent and audible suggestions.

Silent suggestion is of two kinds, Hetro and
Auto, the former meaning suggestion to another,
and the latter meaning suggestion to one's self.
There is greater power in silent suggestion,
whether it be used for right or wrong, than there
is in audible suggestion, because the silent thought
sent to another is subtle, and the recipient knows
nothing of its source, and is often unable to com-
bat it, thinking it originated in his own mind.
Silent suggestion can be used for the benefit of
another so long as it be suggestion, and is not carried to the extent of coercion. For example: You
may have a friend who is likely to give way to
temptation to do wrong. You would have a right
to say to him: "You are good and true; you can
resist that temptation because your own divine
nature has asserted itself." And your friend will
come through his struggle victorious.

You may always suggest mentally to a person
what you have a *right* to say to him audibly—and
it is often inexpedient for you to say audibly what

you have a moral right to say. For example: If a person calls and is taking up more of your time than you can spare, it is morally right for you to say mentally, "Why don't you go?" You have a right to protect yourself from intrusion upon your work. Or perhaps someone has borrowed money from you, and you do not like to ask him to return it though you really need the money. It would be perfectly legitimate for you to say mentally: "Return the money you borrowed." Again, you may be seeking a position and perhaps several other persons are trying to secure the same position. When you are called into the office to state your qualifications, say mentally to the person who is examining you, "You had better give me a chance."

You have a right to help yourself through life by the aid of suggestion, when it is not at the expense of another person; and you have no conception of the number of obstructions this silent power will remove from your path, or how much good you can accomplish with it. Like all other forces, this power grows with use, and you can use silent suggestion legitimately as a moral stimulus. Suppose a person makes a contract with you agreeing to give you certain things in consideration of certain money. After a time you perceive that the contract is not going to be kept by him. You have a right to say mentally to that man,

"You are an honorable man and you want to keep that contract," and in this manner you will create within him a desire to keep it.

Silent suggestion can be used as a defence. For example: When you are conscious that a person is trying to influence you, refuse to accept his suggestions and declare that he cannot accomplish his purpose. This will turn his force back upon himself, and render him impotent to affect you. If you know a person in fiduciary matters is trying to take an advantage of you, commence to work upon his moral nature until you quicken into activity all the latent good there is in him. In this manner you are doing a double good; you are working for yourself and are also bringing out the best in another. But you have no right to coerce another person under any circumstances. You may suggest strongly, forcefully, but not to the extent of coercion, not even to develop the moral nature of another. You may suggest to a friend, "You do not want to drink liquor; you never will get any pleasure from drinking. You do not like the taste of it." And in this manner you may help to destroy his desire and taste for drink; but you have no right to say, "You shall not drink liquor; your hand will be paralyzed when you try to raise a glass of it to your lips; your throat shall close when you try to swallow any intoxicating drink," because such declarations are coercive. Should you succeed in coercing him to stop drinking, you would but hypnotize him, and it would be your will, not his, which would control his appetite and his body; and as soon as your will is removed his taste will reassert itself, and will remain with him till he overcomes it himself. You may help him to overcome his desires, if he wants you to, but you have no right to dominate his will.

You may suggest to a person who owes you, "Give me that money you owe me," but you have no right to say, "You *shall* return to me that money; you shall never sleep again till you have paid me." You have no right to coerce another, either mentally or physically; and though the line of demarkation is very fine, yet it is clear.

It will be well to remember these two rules which may help you in using suggestion. First, when you are suggesting to another to do something for you, speak of yourself as a third person. For example: Suppose Mr. Jones had given you his note, and you wanted him to pay it. He may have given his note to a dozen other persons, and if you were to say mentally to him, "You want to pay that note," he would not know which note was referred to. But if you were to say, "Pay Mr. Blank the note due at such a time," your suggestion would be understood, and very likely be acted upon.

In olden times it was often the custom of physi-

cians to meet their patients with a frown and a dis-
couraging remark; but the modern physician is
beginning to understand the value of suggestion,
and meets his patient with a smile, and the optimistic remark, "You are looking better to-day,
and are feeling better." This is an audible suggestion. Suppose a friend says to you, "I am
feeling miserably," you should reply mentally to
him, "There is no reason why you should not feel
well." If you were to make this statement audibly, after he had declared to the contrary, he
might be offended, because some persons cherish
their ills, and resent a refusal of anyone to recognize them. But the silent, optimistic remark helps
to make positive those who have favorite ills, and
they become hopeful and healthy.

Second, whenever you make a mental suggestion, suggest doubly. Make one suggestion for the
subjective mind and one suggestion for the objective mind, and by doing this your object may be
accomplished in a much shorter time. In suggesting to the subjective mind, tell it the truth; when
you suggest to the objective mind, advise it along
the lines of personal interest. For example: A
man has leased an apartment, but finds the owner
does not intend to keep his agreement to renovate
that apartment. Having a contract, he has a
moral right to insist upon the terms being fulfilled,
and he says mentally to the subjective mind of the

owner of the apartment, "You are an honest man and you will be glad to keep your promise to Mr. Blank." Then say to his objective mind, "It is to your interest to keep your promise with Mr. Blank; he will be a good tenant and it will be a great loss to you to lose him." The man has been told two aspects of the truth, and each aspect appealed to the mind which was able to appreciate and understand it best.

Auto-suggestion is suggesting to yourself, and you should always let the auto-suggestion be made by your higher mind to your lower self. Let the subjective mind give, and the objective receive the suggestion. The greatest objection an Occultist has to hypnotism is that it emphasizes the objective mind, and teaches it to make its dominion stronger over its subjective mind. Suppose you wished to break a habit; you should say to your objective mind, "Now you cannot do that thing again." Sometimes the objective mind will answer, "Why can't I do that?" You should reply "Because it is not to your interest to do it, and you do not want to; you have no desire to; all your desire is gone forever." And the objective mind will begin wondering where the desire has gone, and at that moment accepts the suggestion made; and in this manner you can break any habit if you will but persist in making suggestions.

Deity does not coerce Its children and no child

of God has a right to coerce another, because it is morally wrong to do it. Whatever exists on the mental plane must become embodied upon the material plane sooner or later, and a man's body is a limited expression of his mental traits, as are also the tendencies and habits of his body.

Suppose a mother comes to you, crying, "Save my boy from becoming a gambler!" and you undertake the task of stopping the boy from gaming. You may make your passes, and your mental suggestions, and say: "You shall not gamble any more; you shall suffer an agony of fear every time you attempt to make a wager or touch a card." You may prevent the boy from gambling, but you have not destroyed his love for it, and you have really only delayed his evolution, since he will have to come back to face the same conditions at another time; if not in the same body, then in another one, in a future life, or whenever your will has ceased to control him.

Hypnotism or mental dominion never cures disease; it merely prevents the temporary manifestation of effects. The limitation of its so-called curative power depends upon the will of the hypnotist, and the extent of the hypnosis produced. Henry Wood, in "Practical Ideas," for December, 1900, points out the fact that a percentage of the Christian and Mental Science patients have a recurrence of their diseases within a well-defined period after they are cured. This is because either conscious or unconscious mental dominion was employed by the mind of the practitioner in holding back the manifestation of the trouble; and these returns occur in periods or fractions of seven-year cycles, according to the power of the practitioner. Even though a patient be actually cured, not by mental dominion, but by bringing new elements into his body, unless he puts himself into a new condition of mind and bodily habits, the old disease in course of time is likely to return. On the death of a hypnotist the disease he has held in abeyance usually returns, because the magnetic cord which connects him with his subject is then broken, and, the stronger influence being removed, the weaker mind, with its old line of thinking, reasserts itself.

There is a great limitation in the therapeutical use of hypnotism since its best effects are upon nervous and kindred diseases. In chronic cases, blood diseases, or independent growths within an organism, such as cancers and tumors, it is not successful. In cases of insanity it is more successful, but even there it is subject to limitation. Continuous hypnotic influence upon a patient not only destroys his mental poise and makes him a negative, vacillating creature of impulse, but it also depletes his nerve fluid, and while the operator may seem to temporarily neutralize this weakness, there come great reactions in course of time and the nerves controlling the circulation of the capillary blood vessels become weakened, and the entire circulation becomes irregular and imperfect. Cold hands and feet, with sometimes an intense rush of blood to the head, are the physiological evidences of this condition.

It should not be forgotten that hypnotic influence has a reactionary effect upon the operator. For example, suppose a person attempts to throw his hypnotic influence upon you and you are so positive or your vibrations are so high that his influence fails to affect you, then as a natural operation of law that force which he sent out, not reaching its intended destination, returns to the sender. If it be a malignant force it will do for the sender what it was intended to do for his victim. The greatest crime known to the Great Law is the coercion of an individual center or mind to do evil. No one ever coerced another or used suggestion to the detriment of another; no one ever brought disease or misfortune upon another, that he did not have to drink to the dregs the cup he held to that other's lips. He may escape punishment from the human law, but it will be impossible for him to escape from the Divine Law. In order to send malignant influences to another the sender must hold in his mind the picture of the disaster he wishes to create for the other. It is impossible to do this without creating a matrix in his own aura and this matrix will draw back to the sender just what he has created, for the Great Law works automatically and impartially and irrespective of the fact whether he has succeeded in bringing down disaster upon his victim or not. Did you ever see a person supposed to be a witch or a black magician who was handsome, graceful, happy or wealthy?

Hypnotic influence may last till the operator desires it to be broken or till a stronger will than his, at the request of the subject, shall break it. If a person submits to complete hypnosis but once, in the course of time the influence will become dissipated; but an intense hatred for the operator will become engendered in the heart of the subject when that influence is destroyed, and it will never be eradicated during the lifetime of either. The law works in the same manner in cases of coerced love. If a person succeeds in compelling the love of another through hypnotic influence, that love will turn to the bitterest hatred and then there is nothing that the victim will leave undone to avenge what he believes to be his wrongs. It is right to ask for honest love or to suggest that another person should give you his love; you have a right to picture another's love flowing from him to you, but you have no right to coerce another into loving you. Hypnotic influence can be broken by a person who is stronger than the hypnotist. For example: A may coerce B, but C can break A's influence at B's request even though he is no stronger than A, because C is working for the right and has the Universal Consciousness to aid him.

There are certain conditions of mind which if you will make use of them will make you immune from this malignant force: First. Be mentally positive; then you are not what the hypnotist calls "suggestable." A person who is suggestable is in a passive condition of mind and receives suggestion easily. If you make a practice of concentrating your thoughts upon whatever you are doing, your mind is active and positive and thoughts foreign to you cannot find lodgment with you. Few operators are persistent enough to continue with their suggestions when they fail in reaching the subject after a considerable length of time.

Second. It is accepting the suggestion which enslaves. You cannot prevent the suggestion from coming to you if the operator is persistent, but you need not accept it.

Third. Be on your guard against all suggestions. Examine critically all thoughts that come to you, and test each with this question: "Is it true?" There will be no one who will come in contact with you for many years who will be strong enough to make a suggestion to you and accomplish his purpose immediately. The effort must be repeatedly made before he can succeed. If you examine the thoughts which come to you and find them undesirable, repudiate them and declare you cannot be influenced by them. For example: Suppose you were to suddenly become dissatisfied with your present home. You have always been pleased with it, but suddenly you are seized with a desire to move from that neighborhood and buy somewhere else. Examine those thoughts and ask yourself why you should change your mind without any apparent cause. And if in a few days or weeks a real estate broker meets you and offers a piece of property in the neighborhood you have been thinking of moving into, it may be well for you to consider whether it was his thoughts that have caused your change of mind or whether they were your own.

Fourth. Do not entertain visiting thoughts until you know their character any sooner than you would entertain persons whose character you know nothing about.

Fifth. Select only such thoughts as *you want,* and reject such suggestions as you do not desire. Few people are able to do this, but are constantly being swayed by the influence of those with whom they associate. Other people's manners, words and thoughts mold our lives to a much greater extent than we imagine, and this is because we do not think for ourselves; we do not generate our own thoughts, but accept whatever comes floating along to us. A woman goes shopping. She knows in a general way what she wants, but with her mind full of indefinite thoughts she comes to a positive saleswoman who wants to sell all the goods on her counter. In a vague way the shopper tells the woman she is going to buy a dress and the saleswoman sees an opportunity to dispose of something she is anxious to get rid of. She immediately makes a selection for her customer and impresses her mind with the thought that this is just what she wants. The shopper does not know what she wants, and although this does not seem to be quite the shade or kind of goods she had thought about getting, still she is not sure it would not do. She wavers and the saleswoman sells her the dress, and when it comes home and the positive-minded saleswoman is not present, the woman is disappointed and dissatisfied with her purchase.

A man goes into a restaurant and an obsequious waiter suggests by his manner that a liberal tip is expected. He gives the man no more attention than the proprietor pays him for giving to any other customer, but he wants a tip and he thinks, looks and acts tip till the man cannot, dare not refuse to give it. He is for the moment under the mental dominion of that waiter and even though he be a Judge of the Supreme Court he must yield to the will of a man who perhaps can scarcely write his own name.

That no hypnotist can succeed permanently in life is true. No person can retain possession of a thing gained through black art or by dishonest methods. A thief may seem to prosper for a season but eventually the Great Law will make the proper adjustment and his ill-gotten gains will be swept from him, because Divine Justice does rule the Universe.

LECTURE TEN

THERE is an old saying that "Birds of a feather flock together," which is another way of saying: "Tell me who a man's friends are, and I will tell you what manner of man he is." Through both these maxims the same thought runs—that like mentalities are found in groups. There are certain groupings of forces and of truths; there is also a grouping of minds. Literary people are likely to be drawn together; musicians naturally seek musicians for their friends, and this is due to the fact that the individuals who compose these groups vibrate in the same common key. They think along the same general lines; they have what is sometimes called sympathetic vibration, that is, they vibrate at the same general rate.

In physics we see evidences of sympathetic vibrations. If you strike a note on the piano you will frequently hear a part of a chandelier, or a wine glass on the sideboard vibrate in sympathy with that particular note. This shows that the mass tone of the glass is identical with that of the note upon the piano. In thought there is sympathetic vibration also, and for this reason it is sometimes difficult to determine who is the real inventor of a thing. For example: Who was the inventor of the telephone? If Bell, then why was it necessary to have all the controversy that occurred between him and those claiming it under Gray? Why was it necessary to have a lawsuit and then to compromise their claims? Bell, Gray and Edison were thinking along the same line, had become attached to a certain thought current and developed the same ideas simultaneously.

We often hear the expression: ''I got into a certain current of thought.'' To the careless thinker this expression means nothing in particular, but to the student of Occultism it means a great deal more than a mere form of expression; for there are currents of thought in the great magnetic sea of consciousness in which we live, and we can and do attach ourselves either consciously or unconsciously to different currents with definite results.

Picture to yourself for a moment this magnetic consciousness of which we are a part. It is pulsating with life and is capable of receiving and transmitting thought. In this great magnetic sea there are thought currents as clearly defined as there are currents in the air or in the ocean. You know there is a current in the ocean which is called the Antarctic Drift and another called the Gulf Stream, etc. In Universal Mind there are currents of thought which are as distinctly separate as are these two currents in the ocean; and it is as necessary that we should know about the one as that we should know about the other, because a man draws from the currents in Universal Mind such thoughts or ideas as he is sympathetically vibrating with. When you and I are thinking along the same general line we are in a current of thought, which is one of those in the Universal Consciousness; and because your mind and mine are attached to this current, we are for the time being receiving in unison the same general ideas. Plagiarism may be often explained in this manner. Oliver Wendell Holmes wrote the poem, ''Man Wants but Little Here Below,'' and after it was published a friend called his attention to the fact that Adams had written not only on the same theme, but had used the same similes and many of the same expressions, many years before; yet no one would think of calling Doctor Holmes a plagiarist. By thinking along that line his mind had become attached to the same current of thought that Adams had been in when he expressed himself in a similar manner.

Inventors often get into the same current of thought, and work along similar lines, and then suddenly startle the public with inventions of a like nature, each inventor declaring himself the sole discoverer of the thing invented. During the last two decades or more there has been no great discovery made in physics that can be attributed to the mind of any one man, since several minds have contributed toward each and all the discoveries that have been made. Man draws from the Universal according to his mentality, and groups of men may draw simultaneously the same ideas from the same currents of thought.

These currents of thought are used by men unconsciously, semi-consciously and consciously. For example, a man desires to possess great wealth, and decides he will have it. He knows nothing about the scientific use of mind, but puts certain natural laws into operation through his desire and decision to gain wealth. If he persists, wealth must come to him because he has set the law into operation which will bring it, but it may be a long time coming, because he does not understand how to use his mind scientifically to hasten it. Another man who has studied along the line of Mental Science and who knows there is power in the individual mind to demand from the Universal Mind, says, "Give me wealth." He persists in making his demands frequently and earnestly and in time the wealth will come to him. He has used the law semi-consciously and will obtain what he demands more quickly than the first man. The Occultist knows that by making a mental image of wealth and by concentrating his thoughts upon it he has put into operation a law, and that through the magnetic cord which connects him with his creation he will draw to himself the wealth he has created. He uses the law consciously and therefore realizes his desires much sooner than the other two. To live is to use these currents of force either consciously or unconsciously, but men always attribute their successes to external causes until they learn something about the laws which govern success. At this time many persons are using these Cosmic currents of force for therapeutical purposes and are performing cures of bodily ills through mental processes. Each claims to cure through a system of healing different from the others; as witness Christian Scientist, Mental Scientist, New Thought Scientist, Faith Curer, Divine Healer, the priests of the Water of the Spring of Lourdes, Magnetic Healer, Hypnotists, etc. It makes no difference what the claims of these respective schools may be, the phenomena of healing must be based on the same law. Jesus knew the nature and use of these Cosmic forces, and taught them to his disciples, who produced the phenomena called miracles through the use of them. Apollonius of Tyana and his disciples performed miracles and cures in the same manner; and before these the Essenes, Pythagoreans, Buddhists and Brahmins used these currents of force for the same purposes; and during the early Christian centuries and Middle Ages the Neo-Platonists, Mystics and Rosicrucians used them in their work with mankind.

These currents are Spiritual Forces and are a part of the Universal Spirit or Mind. Spiritual force may be defined as motion generated by Divine Mind in contradistinction to motion generated by individual mind or by mechanical processes. You remember the all-important fact so often reiterated in this course of lectures that the sensitive etheric mind of the Universe is all around us, as air surrounds man or as the ocean surrounds and sustains the fish which live in it. Like the ocean, Divine Mind is always in motion. The ocean has its inherent motion due to the tides, and also its superficial or wave motion due to external causes such as wind, etc. Divine Mind has Its motion, per se, which are the currents within It, and these currents are superficially modified by the thoughts of men. An individual mind cannot permanently work against a Universal current nor misuse it any more than it can keep the tide in the Bay of Fundy from rising; but it can work along the right lines and make use of these great currents to its own advantage, and in this manner work with nature instead of against it.

While it is true that force is one, yet force manifests on this planet under different aspects, and

we will consider five of these as five forces or five
great currents. Remember, all force is one force,
but manifests at different rates of vibration according to the media through which it acts, and
these different rates of vibration we will call, for
convenience' sake, separate currents. Each of
these five currents is subdivided into other currents, and each of these sub-divisions, like the
great currents, is separated from each other by
a difference in their rates of vibration, the same
as the Gulf Stream is separated from the main
body of water through which it flows by a difference in the rate of its vibrations.

These Cosmic currents vibrate red, orange,
green, blue and yellow, and may be pictured as
vibratory currents of color. To illustrate them
crudely we may compare them with physical
things with which we are familiar. The rainbow,
for example. Imagine a great rainbow encircling
the earth, and suppose it to be in motion and you
will have an idea of how these currents look as
they encircle this planet, with each force representing one of the colors of the rainbow—only instead
of the alleged seven colors of the rainbow you will
have five distinct colors. It is true that the real
currents have been partly or dimly seen by men
and are called the zodiacal lights, and the many-
colored Northern Lights also give us glimpses of
portions of these currents, which sweep round and

permeate the earth in every part of it. The Cosmic currents sweep not only over the surface of the ground, but through it, passing down on one side of the globe and up on the other side. They also sweep down and through one side of man and up on the other side, for man is but a small world, and so he and every portion of the world is touched by all these currents. Looking at them from the subjective side of life they appear as if a great number of ribbons of the five different colors were being waved up and down and wound around and around the earth as if all men and living creatures were being entangled in them.

Doubtless you have looked out over the hot pavements of a city in the month of August and have seen the heat vibrations rising from them in wavering clouds. Imagine those grayish white heat vibrations to be of five different colors and you will have a very good picture of how the Cosmic forces look. Suppose my hand were full of ribbon streamers of these different colors and I should shake them rapidly before your eyes; some of you being partially color blind would see only the red and green ribbons, others might see those two colors and the blue, while some would see the yellow and orange and the other three. Each person would see according to his capacity for seeing, and it is the same with your ability to see and use the Cosmic forces. You see and function in the color with which you are connected by reason of your corresponding vibrations. The human mind is related to these currents very much as a telegraph instrument is related to the telegraph wires. It may be attached to any wire and repeat all messages that pass over it. The human mind can attach itself to the blue, the red, the yellow or the green current, as the case may be, and receive everything in that current, and it is through its power to tap the different currents that it is able to draw anything that it may desire from those currents.

You may ask, "How can there be a Cosmic current that we cannot see or feel?" I must call your attention to the fact that because you do not feel or see a force is no reason that it does not exist. You cannot see free electricity and certain conditions must exist before you can see or feel it, yet you do not deny that it is a force and many of you are learning to use it. You do not feel the Cosmic currents because the necessary conditions have not been made to make you feel them. If you were shut in a room where you could not feel the wind and it blew very hard outside, the conditions would not be right for you to feel it, and since it is a force which cannot be seen you would not know that it existed.

The first thing to do to become conscious of these color currents is to image or visualize them, and remember that nothing was ever imagined by mind that does not exist in the Universe. If you are vibrating green and the blue has begun to tinge your aura then visualize the blue and it will be drawn into you, since whatever you concentrate upon or image you must draw to yourself. If you have developed to the point of the blue vibration tinged with the yellow then you can draw the yellow Cosmic current into yourself. And whenever you are able to draw to you a current that is vibrating higher than your predominating color you raise your own vibrations and receive all the good that you are capable of assimilating from that current. These mental pictures and concentration are the two instruments we utilize for the purpose of connecting ourselves with Cosmic currents which are constantly flowing around the earth.

If it is difficult for you to image or visualize the color you desire then secure a bit of ribbon of the proper shade, or a drapery of the color you want and look at it until you have the color impressed upon your mind. This will help you to visualize the Cosmic currents, and when you are concentrating you should realize that they are currents of force, though you speak of them in terms of color. When the blue current is mentioned that force is meant which vibrates at a rate that makes it appear as blue. Electricity is a part of this current and when the proper mechanism is used to condense and conduct it, it manifests as blue to the physical eyes.

Commencing with the red current we will study that first because it is lowest in the scale. Red vibrations in anything mean emotion of some sort. In man it indicates that his animal nature is in the ascendency; in animals it is a perfectly natural vibration but can be stimulated by external suggestions to an ungovernable or furious extent. For example; the bull or turkey gobbler are often driven into a frenzy of rage at sight of a red rag. This is because the color red makes a picture in the mind of the creature and by looking at that picture its mind becomes connected with the Universal current of red. Having "tapped" that force it draws into itself all that it can assimilate of that rate of vibration and is angry. Man, like the animal, sometimes uses the red current unconsciously and whenever he gets angry he connects himself with it whether conscious of it or not, and this is the reason he loses his self-control so quickly. As soon as he becomes enraged his aura changes to the vibration red; then his aura is vibrating sympathetically with the red Cosmic current and the connection between the two is instantly made. The red current has been tapped, the man's aura is the conducting instrument for that force and immediately the man becomes filled with that vibration. Self-control is swept away and he rages like a mad animal. He has connected himself with everybody in the world who is angry at that moment and he is functioning in these vibrations. He is receiving telepathically all the ugly things that other angry people are thinking about, and he does things while in that condition which he had never before thought of doing. If he commits murder while in this angry condition the legal fraternity call him emotionally insane and he escapes capital punishment by being incarcerated in an aslyum for a while. Red is a low, disruptive, jagged vibration, and when it is drawn into a person it begins its disruptive work upon the physical body of that person, and all the good creations which he has made are instantly repelled from his aura. And not only are good things and good people repelled from him, but he attracts all the so-called evil manifestations and unless he recovers his mental poise and gets out of that red current nothing but misfortune will come until he is swept out of his body.

Anger demagnetizes the atoms which compose the physical body. There is a positive and a negative side to every atom as there is to every magnetic thing in the world. When we speak of a body having magnetic polarity we mean that to the negative of one side stands the positive of the next and that to the negative of one atom stands the positive side of another atom; and when the body is demagnetized this relationship is destroyed.

The higher forces of nature flow rhythmically over these atoms when they are magnetically polarized; but when the red current, which is repellent, enters a body it demagnetizes the atoms and prepares a condition for bacteria to enter and disease to follow. Sometimes the body becomes instantly disrupted by this demagnetizing force and apoplexy is caused. Many times paralysis is produced because the red force is so great that the atoms which compose the nerves of the body become demagnetized and never afterward regain their polarity. Different shades of the red compose the sub-currents of the great red current. The light shade, called scarlet, indicates anger; the darker shade, called crimson, indicates sex desire. Fear is indicated by a still darker shade, which is a red-brown and which sometimes deepens to almost a brown-black, and the sense gratification is represented by a shade of wine color.

The Occultist uses this red current solely for the purpose of restoring the sex functions in a person who has become depleted and who desires to use his powers solely in a creative manner. The black magicians use the red current for the purpose of destruction, for that force can be utilized to destroy and it can also be used to precipitate anything upon the material plane which floats or lives within it. In Black Magic it is used for producing pests, plagues and all kinds of diseases. The White Magician can use it when the law requires or when mankind may be helped thereby, as Moses the Occultist and the Egyptian magicians used it when Egypt was made to suffer for her sins.

The orange current or force is used by everything that lives upon this earth. It is the life current and sustains every plant and animal that exists. Every creature that breathes inhales it with the atmosphere, and things that do not have lung capacity absorb this great force through their bodies as sponges absorb water or moisture. If an animal becomes ill it immediately goes out into the sunlight and breathes deeply of this orange force and if permitted to remain in the sunshine and all drugs, such as our sometimes unwise veterinary surgeons give to animals, are withheld the creature will get well.

The Occultist uses this life force in treating animals, young children and undeveloped persons who have not reached the point in their evolution where they vibrate green. He also uses it in stimulating the growth of plants. The Indian Yogi puts a seed into the earth and then condenses this orange force into it with such intensity that while you stand looking at him the plant is forced out of the soil, comes to maturity and bears fruit before your eyes. This wonderful feat is imitated by sleight of hand performers and by hypnotists who deceive people into believing they see it done. But there are men who can and do produce this phenomenon and it is done by using the orange current in the manner I have described.

Green is the current of individualization. It also represents selfishness both in its higher and its lower forms. Manifesting in this great current is all desire for personal possessions, distinctions and individual aggrandizement. It is the current of intellectualization without intuition. There are many people who have a great deal of book learning, whose objective minds are trained and who are intellectual, and their memory of facts and alleged facts is wonderful; but their subjective minds may be altogether undeveloped, and yet these persons pass for very wise individuals. They vibrate green and have but little or no real knowledge. For example, a lawyer may know thoroughly the laws of the State of New York and may know exactly what decision has been given in a similar case to any proposition you may submit to him; but to-morrow the legislature may meet and do away with all the old statutes and pass a new set of laws and the lawyer's knowledge would be legislated out of existence.

There may be what we call intellectualization of a very high order and yet it does not rise above the green current.

Selfishness in its lowest aspect is in a sub-current and belongs in the shade called bottle-green. The desire for personal possessions, for distinction and for aggrandizement is the color of the grass we see in the Autumn, is a very pronounced shade, but not so dark as the bottle-green. Intellectualization without intuition is a still lighter shade and a wise individualization without selfishness is of the shade called pastel-green.

Individualization manifests as the green vibration everywhere in the Universe and when you look out into the heavens at night and see a star sending forth a green light you may know that it, like our earth, is passing through the period of individualization, and like our own world, is the fourth planet in a chain of seven. The planet of individualization is where Men or Minds become self-dependent, independent, self-reliant. The grass and foliage upon our earth is green because in the vegetable kingdom Universal Consciousness is making an effort to individualize. The keynote of our world is Fa, which corresponds to the green color and which produces it by its vibration. Animal souls are of this color at birth, but soon take the deeper color red when their bodies become strong enough to express desire for procreation.

As man develops and becomes more and more individualized he vibrates green in proportion to his development.

The Occultist uses this color to create for himself and for others wealth, honor, position and every material thing that can be desired. Suppose he desires to make a material creation, he would concentrate upon the green current until every part of his entire being was vibrating green or until he had connected himself with this current. After making his connection he would select the sub-current he desired and in that make the mental picture of the thing to be created. Suppose he wanted some money, he would know that the financial current, which is a part of the green current, was the one to use. After making his connection and the picture of the amount he wants he will no longer think of the color current, but will put all his force in concentrating upon his creation, and the Great Consciousness will bring his creation to him out of this green current. The Occultist gets quicker results than unconscious users of this law because he does not waste his force, but goes directly and scientifically to work. He knows what he wants and how to get it and there is no uncertainty or indecision in his efforts, and as a consequence no delay.

In cases of nervousness, the Occultist uses green to individualize and strengthen the nerves, and when he draws this vibration into the body of a patient he brings in new materials and new atoms which give new life. For failing eyesight and most eye troubles, green is the proper current to use since the optic nerves are revitalized and individualized by its strengthening vibrations. The Occultist also uses this current as an antidote for altruism. There comes a time in the career of every man in some life when he feels that he must be an Atlas and go about carrying the world on his back. He wants to bear everybody's sorrows and thinks it a great privilege to give away everything he has in the world. He becomes a devout believer in poverty and piety and sometimes goes so far as to study the pictures of Jesus of Nazareth and of the martyrs and trims his beard to look like theirs, that he may look the life of sacrifice he tries to live. He dissipates himself mentally, physically and financially and sooner or later nervous prostration if not starvation claims his body, and he goes out upon the next plane of consciousness. For such a person the Occultist uses the green current to restore him to a normal condition of individualization.

The Occultist is taught never to give more of anything than his surplus, and never to assume the burdens of another, for by so doing he would be robbing that other of the experience he came into this world to get. In every walk of life we see people who have assumed burdens that do not belong to them and who are crying aloud to Deity for help and are demanding to know why such burdens should be laid upon their shoulders. God never laid upon any of His children anything that was greater than they could bear; and when we find our accumulations of sorrow and care becoming too great to endure, it is time to examine the bundle and see if we have not taken something that does not belong to us, for a mistaken sense of duty more often leads us into difficulties than a real duty does.

The color blue represents all the higher mental qualities. In the sub-currents are literature, music, art, the higher education, organization, order, form, harmony, etc. This force can never be used by animals, but only by the subjective mind of man. All inspiration along any line of thought is due to the inflow of this blue current, of which men are many times entirely unconscious. Artists in any line express greater things than are in their own minds to express. We often hear it said of another, "He taught better than he knew." This kind of work has been called inspirational, but the real source of inspiration has never been understood or explained. One man believes the soul of his departed wife inspired him to write the burning lines of verse that made him famous. Another thinks an old Master stood behind him

while he knelt and in the deepest reverence painted
his best picture. The musician's soul thrills with
the melody that he alone can hear and he tells you
in a whisper that the angels came, while he sat
alone, and played such symphonies as were never
heard on earth before and that in his poor, stum-
bling way he had tried to reproduce them on his
instrument. And none of these knew he had
been unconsciously connected through concentration with the blue Cosmic current and had received
from it a few of the gems that are stored therein.

Suppose you desire to be a musician; the indigo
blue sub-current is the one you should connect
yourself with. All great composers have taken
their inspiration from this current and it was according to each one's capacity to draw into himself this force and listen to "the music of the
spheres," that made him the musician that he
was. The musical currents run from the deep
indigo blue to the sky blue, but no one known to
the world has yet been able to reach the highest
sub-current and to bring from it the music that
lies there. That soul is yet to come and will be the
gift of the twentieth century to the world. But
each and every one can draw inspiration to himself
that will enable him to understand, to interpret,
to execute and to compose music according to his
own development.

The sub-current for literature is a light blue—

the blue we see in the Autumn sky. Anyone can write if he will be persistent enough to become a good grammarian, master the technicalities of rhetoric and learn to tap the universal current in which the gems of this art are stored. In each human soul lies latent the ability to learn every art and science which is known; and by aid of these great currents and sub-currents to become perfect in his knowledge of all.

The Occultist uses the blue current also for restoring harmony and health to persons who are beginning to have a tinge of blue beyond the green. Persons who vibrate between the blue and green are passing in their development from where the objective mind no longer has entire dominion over the subjective, but shares with it the honors of controlling the body and its mundane affairs.

Yellow is the highest color vibration upon this planet and is therefore the greatest force. It is Spiritual and Creative Love. It is Wisdom, Intuition, Divine Harmony and is the highest aspect of Deity that we are capable of understanding at this time. It embraces all the spiritual qualities we can conceive, and I regret to say that man does not possess very many of them as yet. To acquire this force man must develop to the point where the subjective mind controls the objective, and when he can attach himself to the yellow Cosmic current he can accomplish anything he may undertake to do upon this planet. An undeveloped person cannot use the yellow current of force because it is a vibration so much higher than his own that there is no sympathy between him and it; and it can be used to help only such persons as are in sympathy with it.

In using the Cosmic currents for healing, the Occultist takes the left hand of the patient in his right hand, and after drawing into himself the current he desires to use he passes it out through his right hand into the left side of his patient. The left side, being the receptive side, the patient receives this force without difficulty; and it passes down his left side and up the right and round and over and through his body until every nerve and fiber of his body is soothed and relaxed by this wonderful divine force. But one should not forget the caution given on page 206 about depleting one's self. A knowledge of these forces and how to use them gives one almost unlimited power; for, where the human will alone and unaided is unable to accomplish its purpose, it can by putting into operation these universal forces have Omnipotence working with it, making an assured success of its every undertaking.

LECTURE ELEVEN

DISEASE is, as the name indicates, dis-ease, and means an absence of ease. Pathologically speaking, according to one of the definitions of the Century Dictionary, disease is a "deviation from the healthy or normal condition of any of the functions or tissues of the body," and therefore it is necessary to ascertain what the normal condition of the body is before we may know when it is in a diseased or abnormal condition, and to know this we must learn how the body is builded.

Starting with its lowest aspect we find that the physical body is made up of a great number of little individual lives which the modern physicist calls atoms. These atoms group and form what is called molecules. A number of these molecules grouped together form a complex individual life which is called a cell and the grouping together of a number of cells forms an organ, tissue, muscle, etc., and a combination of the necessary muscles, tissues, organs, bones and fluids, forms a mass or body which has a common rate of vibration and a shape.

Did you ever stop to think why your physical body holds its form? Why should not your arm fly off into space in one direction while a foot goes in another direction? It is because there is a dominant mass vibration which holds together the different portions of the body responding to it. The earth is held together by the law of gravitation; there is a mass tone which holds its component parts together as one, and so long as that vibratory force continues to play upon this planet there can never be a disintegration of it. In the same way each person has his own personal law of gravitation or mass vibration which holds all the parts of his body together.

This magnetic force, personal law of gravitation or mass vibration of the body, is the vibration of the objective mind which ensouls it. Its normal color should be green, but the development of the man determines the color at any time in his evolution; and in the earlier stages of his development, when his desires and passions are dominant, his vibrations drop lower than the green and he becomes a dirty brown.

The objective mind gives the physical body its shape, and it is because of the presence of the mind in the body that the particles, which come from all sources to make up the magnetic sphere, group themselves into the form of the physical man. You have placed a horse-shoe magnet over a quantity of steel filings and have seen them rush together and crowd themselves around the magnet, taking its form. The atoms, like the steel filings, are drawn to the magnet mind and though they come from earth, air, food and water they are held together in the position they occupy by the mass vibration of the objective mind.

While there is a mass vibration, still each organ has an individual modification of this vibration, otherwise it could not be an organ separate and distinct from the rest of the body; and while each organ responds as it were to the dominant tone it also has its sub-tone. In the liver, for example, there is the orange life force which has drawn together all the particles which compose that organ. The blood passing through the liver has a tendency to modify the orange vibrations with its own, which is red. The dominant note of the objective mind, which is green, holds together this mass of red and orange vibration because it is higher and therefore stronger, and you have the three colors blended together in a mass of mixed vibrations which make brown. The color of the liver seen subjectively looks very much as it does objectively.

When the vibration of the objective mind is the controlling or dominant vibration of all the organs of the physical body then it is in a normal or healthy condition. Disease is the lowering, below the normal, of the vibrations of a part or of all the body—except in cases of disruption or misplacement of bones or other parts of the body. For illustration we will take the liver again, which has its own separate organic, complex existence by reason of its construction. Its cells are held together by the orange organic vibration, yet these vibrations are modified and controlled by the higher mass vibration of the objective mind; now suppose the liver instead of responding to the higher mass vibrations, gradually begins to lose them and takes a lower rate of vibration, then you have what is called a torpid liver.

Diseases manifest in one of two general ways. First, where the vibration of an organ is itself lowered and it manifests disharmony within itself; and second, where the vibration of an organ is lowered and it becomes demagnetized sufficiently to permit foreign atoms to enter and set up an independent action. The first condition, if it be not corrected, will cause disintegration or disruption of the entire organ; the second condition results in great relaxation with large interstices between the atoms, where foreign elements enter and set up a disharmonious separate organization, as for example in tuberculosis, cancer or tumor.

Occultism teaches that all disease has its root or origin in ignorance. The reason persons do not have long lives is because they do not know how to live. It is reported that Professor Loeb, Dr.

Matthews and others think that if we could discover the proper electrical conditions we could
prolong the human life to more than two hundred
years. It is said by physicists that most animals
live about five times as long as is required for
them to mature. Applying this rule to man he
ought to live to be at least one hundred and five
years old. That he does not live to this age is
because he does not understand the laws of life
and the real nature of disease. He knows nothing
about controlling the atoms which compose his
body nor how to use the Cosmic forces with which
he is constantly surrounded for the purpose of
revivifying his physical body. "The wages of sin
(ignorance) is death," and disease is the result
of mental conditions.

For example, take a common cold. In ninety-
nine cases out of one hundred, colds are contracted when people are mentally negative. The
mind, instead of being positive, instead of dominating its physical particles and holding them
contracted into a proper shape, becomes relaxed
and negative and loses its force. As a consequence, the body responds to this relaxed condition, the molecules become abnormally separated,
and foreign elements enter, and set up an independent activity of their own. The cause was
mental relaxation, or negativeness.

Why does a piece of glass receive the impression from the point of a diamond when the diamond will not receive an impression from the glass? Because the diamond is of a quick, positive, high rate of vibration, while the glass is negative and of a much slower rate than the diamond. The glass cannot enter the interstices of the diamond because of its intense vibration. Thus it is with the mind that is positive and strong; it can dominate and control its body so well that foreign destructive elements cannot enter into it.

Some diseases can be traced back to the mental conditions which produced them and some cannot. Many cases of heart trouble are directly traceable to fear. The mind, working upon the body, causes an irregular flow of blood; the fear, with its concomitant heart disturbance, commences a vibration of an abnormal rate, and soon that condition, which, in the beginning was a functional trouble, becomes organic disease. Many fevers are due to fear. The first thing you should do for a patient who is suffering with fever is to take away his fear, and his temperature will drop degrees at a time. The cause of congestion of different organs of the body can often be traced back to a violent paroxysm of anger. Professor Elmer Gates, of Washington, D. C., has found that a large number of acids and poisons in the blood are created by the direct action of the mind.

Sometimes the mental cause cannot be traced,

because there have been several different mental
conditions which combined to produce the material result. Then, too, a disease is often produced
mentally, and before it appears physically other
mental conditions have arisen which prevent its
being traced to its original cause. Occultism goes
so far as to declare that even the so-called heredi-
tary diseases are due to the mental condition of
the sufferer, because it is the mental condition or
quality of the mind during a previous incarnation,
which brought him into that particular family,
and compelled him to take the diseased body at
birth.

Disease may be divided into two classes, the
imaginary and the real. Imaginary disease is a
picture held firmly by the objective mind, which
causes more or less physical correspondence. This
kind of disease is often created in total disregard
of the laws governing anatomy or physiology; and
is the hardest to cure, because persons possessed
of it hold to it so persistently that an entire revi-
sion of their mode of thought must be made before
it can be cured. It is not at all infrequent to have
a patient complain of kidney disease, locating the
pain and the organs several inches below the waist
line. The spleen is often supposed to be on the
right side of the body, and phantom tumors appear and disappear. But all these mental pictures, if held long enough, create matrices or

vortices, and draw into them the elements that will bring finally the actual disease that was at first purely imaginary. For example: Sometimes indigestion and gases in the stomach cause a distention of that organ, it presses up against the heart region, causing a functional disturbance of the heart, and the patient becomes convinced that he has organic heart disease. This picture in the patient's mind is the matrix, and his fear of the disease draws it to him in course of time. If the mind holds the picture of anything long enough, whether it be disease or health, poverty or prosperity, that picture must and will materialize. You who have followed Charcot's experiments need no further proof of the action of the mind upon the body.

The second class or real disease, produced primarily by mental causes, and often supplemented by a proximate physical cause, must be cured by controlling the imaging faculty. And in this connection let it be understood that the words "cure" and "heal" are used as popularly understood, and will be used interchangeably—not in any specialized sense, as some modern metaphysicians use them. To cure real disease is to restore to a normal condition the functions or tissues of the body, and to do this the vibrations of the affected part must be raised to their normal rate. In cases of misplacement, dislocation, or broken bones, the quickest way to obtain relief is to send for a competent physician or an anatomist and have an adjustment made of the injured member or organ. In cases of disruption of blood vessels, or muscles, a surgeon's aid should be immediately sought; not because mind is unable to cure any or all of these cases, but because of the fact that at the present time, even among educated people, mind is many times impotent through misuse or non-use. Mental treatment should follow these physical treatments in order to obviate unnecessary suffering and to obtain rapid recovery.

In cases where the vibrations of a part of the body have been lowered, or where foreign particles have entered, there are several material methods of restoring health or harmony to the affected parts. One of these is stimulation by physical manipulation, as in the practice of Osteopathy; another is stimulation through electrical appliances. Neither of these methods, however, reaches the mental cause for the disease, and even though the physical disturbance be removed through either method, it can be only a question of time before it reappears. The electric current is a part of the Cosmic blue current, and by intelligent use it may be made to raise the vibrations of an affected part and restore it to its normal condition; unaided by mind, it can only remove the effects, and never the cause of the disease. The time is not far distant when the two great therapeutical agencies for healing the sick will be electricity and manipulation, representing the material school, and mind, representing the metaphysical school.

A third means of curing disease is by properly prepared non-poisonous vegetable compounds. The Occultist does not believe in the use of mineral drugs as now practiced, nor does he believe that poisons should be administered to a patient. Most minerals and poisons are of such a low rate of vibration that when introduced into the physical body they serve to finally lower its vibrations rather than to raise them. Though they stimulate temporarily, the reaction leaves the patient in a worse condition. Poisons sometimes appear to effect a cure because upon their administration the acute form of the disease disappears; but even a close study of effects teaches us that the disease was not cured; its expression was changed, but it soon appeared in another form and place, and a new name had to be invented to designate it from the old one. To deny that drugs have an effect upon the human body, as do some of the radical metaphysicians at the present time, is to deny and ignore the observations of daily life, and also the law of physics, which asserts that two or more bodies coming into juxtaposition mutually affect each other; and also excludes consciousness from a part of the Universe. Yet these same metaphysicians eat food to sustain their physical bodies, while denying that matter affects matter.

The mineral kingdom supports the vegetable kingdom, and the latter supports the animal kingdom; and according to the natural order of things, it is unreasonable to pass over and ignore as impotent the very kingdom that supplies our food, and to go among the minerals for our medicines. The vegetables used for remedies must be properly and scientifically compounded, however, if the best results are to be had from their use; but the same care must also be observed with the preparation of our food. In Materia Medica there is never an allowance made for a difference in the vibrations of persons who are being treated. A man vibrating green would receive the same prescription from a physician that one would receive who was vibrating red or brown. This is the reason modern medicine is what it is called, an experimental science. When a vegetable remedy has been suitably compounded for an individual according to his vibrations, a cure will be effected by that remedy. Then the same medicine, if it were given to another person suffering from the same disease, but whose vibrations were of a totally different rate or color, would have a different effect. The vibrations of the vegetable remedies must supplement the lowered vibrations of the person using them, if good results are to be had.

Let it be understood, however, that Occultism teaches that mind is the supreme power, and, when properly developed and trained, can cure all diseases, and that in the course of time it will be the only force that man will use to keep the human body in a normal, healthy and harmonious condition. But until that Arcadian time shall come, it is not well to deny that the Great Consciousness has also provided for Its undeveloped children material ways and means for their relief from physical ills.

In curing disease by the power of mind there is the conscious and the unconscious use of the Cosmic forces. All the modern metaphysical schools differ somewhat among themselves in regard to the process by which cures are performed, yet all perform some remarkable ones. Some schools use strenuous denials, and, consciously or unconsciously, hypnotize their patients, and while the patients are in this condition change their thought, and in this manner change the manifestation of the disease they are suffering from. Other schools, through repeated suggestion, cause the patient to accept a new line of thought, and with the change of thought the body changes. In both these classes of cases it is the direct action of mind upon mind which brings

about the change in the condition of the patients.
Other schools, through denials and affirmations,
or through affirmations and demand, petition or
prayer, and through picturing the desired result,
unconsciously put into operation the Cosmic
forces. The Occult school uses consciously the
Cosmic forces for the purpose of healing. In the
two last-named schools there is not only the action
of mind upon mind, but new elements are drawn
into the physical body of the patient, whereby the
old, diseased atoms are cast out and new ones are
left in their places.

There are three things that the Occultist attempts to do in making a cure through mental
means. First, he destroys the mental picture of
disease which his patient holds as a matrix; second, he raises the vibrations of that portion of the
body which has become lowered, and makes it
vibrate normally, thus forcing out all foreign
elements; and third, he supplements the elements
driven out with new elements, which are introduced into the system by the Cosmic force flowing
through it.

Here are a few rules that may be helpful to
you in demonstrating over disease: First. It is
well to avoid seeing the manifestation of the disease, if possible.

By doing this you will not have the picture of
disease constantly in mind and will be able to see

more clearly the picture of perfect health you must create for the patient. If you do not see the objective symptoms of an ugly wound, or an artificial growth, it is easier to make a perfect image and to present that picture to the mind of the patient. In cases where there are only subjective symptoms, never let your sympathies go out to the patient, but hold yourself positive against any emotion of fear which he may have. The moment your own emotions become joined with his, your power to destroy his mental pictures of disease is weakened; you have then accepted his creations and are but accentuating the pictures in his mind.

Second. When you have learned from the patient what his creations are, you are able to destroy them by denying their permanency, if they exist temporarily, or by denying them absolutely if they are imaginary.

After making your denials, follow them with affirmations of that which is true; create a perfect physical condition for your patient, and hold that thought picture till he himself accepts it. Should a patient come to you claiming heart disease, when the physical disturbance was nothing but indigestion, do not deny his claim audibly lest he be offended. It is not necessary to give a patient a diagnosis of his actual condition, because sometimes this would but intensify his fears.

In actual disease deny its permanency and affirm

health. For example, in case of a cold, deny its permanency and declare positiveness for the patient, and as his vibrations are raised, direct the Cosmic force through his body. As his relaxed condition is corrected and the interstices between the atoms grow smaller, the foreign elements become crowded out or expelled from the system; and under this treatment every part of the body will respond to the positive condition of your mind. Denials destroy; affirmations create. The Christian Scientists, and many Mental Scientists use denials largely and sometimes exclusively, while the New Thought Scientists use affirmations alone. It is urged by this last-named class of healers that the denial is contained in the affirmation; but to mentally affirm a healthy condition without denying or destroying the pictures of disease held by the patient, is like attempting to build a new house on a site already occupied by another building without first clearing the ground. You could take out an old brick and put a new one in its place till the new house was built; but it would require a much longer time than it would to tear down the old structure first.

Third. In ordinary treatment by physical contact, take the left hand of your patient with your right hand, that the Cosmic Force may enter your left side and pass out at your right, or positive side, into the left, or receptive side, of the patient.

You should remain in a positive condition of mind while treating in this manner, or your own personal magnetism or life force will be drawn from you with the Cosmic Force into the patient.

Fourth. In a case of depleted mental condition of a patient, in epilepsy, insanity, and in spinal trouble, place your right hand upon the top of the patient's head while giving the treatment. This position throws the current where it is most needed, and the results will be more nearly immediate.

Fifth. In cases of cancers, tumors, boils, swellings, or any kind of separate growth, cover the affected part with a white silk handkerchief, and then place your right hand over it while giving the treatment.

The object in doing this is twofold. First, by covering the growth with the handkerchief, you do not see it and are better able to picture perfection in its place; and second, by placing your hand upon the affected part you bring the current of force directly into it, and this conserves force.

Sixth. Keep your left hand off the patient when treating.

Otherwise you form a complete circuit with him, and as the new life goes into him through his left hand or side, you draw his old, worn-out or demagnetized atoms into yourself, thereby lowering your own rate of vibration, and bringing a physical condition upon yourself similar to that which you are trying to relieve.

Seventh. In separate growths, use the highest shade of the particular Cosmic Force or color you have selected to use for your patient.

Suppose you desire to use green; then treat with the ultra ray of green, because that is the highest rate of vibration of that color and will bring the quickest results. Herein lies the great success of the Occultist over the majority of healers, and over those who use mechanical processes. When the X-ray—which is now known to be one of the higher shades of green—is thrown upon an individualized growth, it immediately commences its disruptive process, and much better results are obtained than with the knife. Its limitation is like that of surgery, in that it does not reach the blood; consequently, if the germs are through the blood of the patient, there will be a return of the disease. But if the healer places his hand over the affected part and uses the ultra shade of the Cosmic color selected, and directs the current through the entire system, the germs will be destroyed, and a return of the disease will be impossible.

Eighth. Concentrate on the aura of the patient to get his predominant color, and then ask of the Universal Consciousness that the color may be made known to you.

This should be done in case you are not clairvoyant, and do not see Cosmic colors at will. Through this practice you will learn to sense the color or vibration of a person as you sense his character.

Ninth. Demand of Deity that you may be used as an instrument for It to manifest through.

This demand, like any other, must, and will be, met, because whatever is held in mind constantly must sooner or later materialize. If you desire to be a healer of the sick, and to relieve suffering, that thought in your mind makes of you that kind of a center, and if you are honest and faithful all the healing powers in the Universe will flow through you in order that your demands may be fulfilled. It is the mental condition which draws or repels Cosmic Force, and the better life you live, the purer your thoughts, and the higher your aspirations, the more perfectly can Cosmic forces be used by you to restore health to others.

Tenth. Always treat yourself for positiveness before treating a patient.

According to your own positiveness can you be a channel or center through which Cosmic forces can flow. Declare mentally something like this: "Divine Force is made manifest in me. I am positive, positive, positive. I have the power to destroy sickness and ignorance." This declaration will raise your own vibrations and make you a better instrument. If you are not positive, your own animal magnetism is likely to pass from you to your patient, and you will be left in a depleted condition. Another reason for becoming positive before commencing to treat a patient is that you may not take upon yourself the pains or disease from your patient, as so many metaphysicians do.

Eleventh. Always use the color, or shade of the color, next higher in the scale of vibration than the predominating color of your patient.

Suppose you are going to treat a person who vibrates in the higher shade of green. Then use the blue Cosmic Force, which he must respond to, but which he will react from. But by using a color higher than his normal one, you raise his vibrations and when the reaction comes he will not go below the highest shades of his own color; and the relief he receives will be permanent.

Twelfth. Realize that these Cosmic forces are manifesting as vibrations or color. Do not think of them as color merely. Let their force aspect be predominant in your mind and when treating with them, picture them as sparkling vibrations flowing into you, and through you into your patient.

Thirteenth. Use suggestion as a supplemental aid to the treatment by color.

Use it for the purpose of destroying in the mind of your patient the picture of disease, and for creating a new picture of health. For example: First get the full name of your patient, and then

call him mentally by that name until you feel you
have his attention. Remember, everyone must receive every thought that is repeatedly sent to him
—whether he accepts it or not is another matter.
If your patient has a pet name, one that he hears
most at home, use that until he is listening to what
you have to say. We will suppose he is called Jim
Smith. You should say, ''Jim Smith, you are
mind, and, being mind, you cannot be diseased.''
Immediately you have made a distinction in the
patient's mind between his mind—himself—and
his body; and now you have his mind working
with you to establish the physical condition you
desire. Then say: ''Your body is constantly
changing, but you are mind, and can control your
body; you can draw new atoms, new life into yourself, and health can be restored.'' Suggest the
power to control and to bring health. With every
treatment say: ''You have no fear of disease because you know you are getting well.'' It is best
to repeat each of these suggestions slowly several
times in order that the patient may grasp them
fully, and when you have removed the demagnetizing low vibrations of fear, the higher vibrations of
health will flow into the patient. Destroy fear and
all feverish conditions disappear. Suppose the
patient has consumption of the lungs. Fear that
he has an incurable disease is the first thing to
remove from his mind; then image for him the

picture of perfect lungs with the Cosmic Force flowing through them and use such suggestions, denials and affirmations as your intuition directs.

Fourteenth. Use as few words as possible to express your thoughts.

The more clearly and concisely your ideas are expressed the more easily will they be impressed upon the mind of the patient. Instead of saying: "God is love and you are a manifestation of His idea and therefore cannot express anything but love," and instead of giving a philosophical explanation of the relationship between God and the patient, and showing how God will answer his prayers for help and health, say something short and decisive, such as "You are not afraid of this disorder; you cannot be afraid, because it is nothing to fear. You are getting well. You are mind and can control your body."

These are a few of the rules and suggestions which may be used in successful mind healing. There are others, but I am now trying to show you those which exemplify the laws which underlie the phenomena of healing. There is a law which lies behind form and if you understand and practice these suggestions I have made, you can gradually change the rates of vibration of your body and also its form until you can make it precisely what you desire. Through this practice will come the power to help others, for with every effort you will grow stronger.

By attending a course of twelve lectures on harmony you will not become a great musician, but you may in those lectures be taught how to study and how to practice. It is by diligent practice that proficiency in anything can be attained, and so it is with Occultism. It is the regular mental practice, the use of Cosmic forces, the imaging, the controlling, the directing, the thinking that make you strong. Having given you the rules it remains with you whether this knowledge shall be purely intellectual or whether you will make practical use of it.

LECTURE TWELVE

In the preceding lectures you were taught how to acquire spiritual perception and mental qualities through the use of Cosmic forces. You have also been taught how, by the power of Divine Mind, to use your mental forces, not only for your own benefit, but for the benefit of others; and now, having learned something about the spiritual and mental planes of being we shall take into consideration the third and last plane. This is where man acquires or fails to acquire an abundance of worldly goods, and where he must understand something about the law of Opulence if he is to succeed. Since many persons believe the possession of material wealth is as essential to happiness as is the possession of perfect health, and since there are no accidents in the world and every detail of our lives is governed by law, it seems absolutely necessary that we should thoroughly understand the law governing Opulence, so that we may control our finances instead of becoming victims of circumstances.

If you have not possessions then it is because

you have not used the law of Opulence for your own benefit. It is a well known fact in Occultism that everyone has now just what he deserves, and this is as true relative to Opulence as it is to spiritual and mental qualities. But before we discuss the law of Opulence in itself let us consider certain other aspects of the law of evolution which may have a bearing on what I shall say later.

If you have studied the creatures in the animal kingdom you know how a mother bird will work to feed her young until they reach a certain age, but when the time has come for each little bird to work for his individual self, she crowds them all out of the nest and throws each one upon his own responsibility. Other animals are devoted to the care of their young until they reach a certain age and then desert them or quarrel with and drive them away to learn independence and to act for themselves. A wise man gives to his child a proper education and training during the years when its character is forming; but when it reaches its majority he sends it forth to assume the responsibility it must assume if it is to become individualized. And the great Universal Consciousness, Father–Mother, during the first part of the evolutionary period on a planet, stands behind man as the evolutionary impulse pushing him onward in his career until he develops to the point where he becomes self-reliant. Then this impulse is withdrawn and from that time on man must develop through his own inherent force, and through a knowledge of the laws of nature and their uses.

According to the Occultist's estimate such first part of the cycle of this planet was reached in 1898; at that time the childhood of the race ended. Before that the evolutionary law provided for Its children, but since that date the Cosmic Consciousness has been gradually relaxing Its effort, and henceforth each individual must learn to rely upon his own strength and knowledge of law for his success in life. This may seem cruel at first thought, but it is really kind and just, because it gives each man an opportunity to develop his best qualities.

It is of the greatest importance that we who represent principles somewhat in advance of the race should realize that all things are governed by law and that not one of the least of these is the law of Opulence. Deity does not give attributes or things to us because we are good. It does not give opulence as a reward for Spiritual acquirement; but if we want Spiritual qualities we must use certain laws to receive spiritual things, and if we want material things we must use the laws which govern the distribution of them.

In the first part of the period which ended in 1898 the old Adamic curse was upon humanity. "In the sweat of thy face shalt thou eat bread." But as the race advanced in evolution some men came from under that curse and were able consciously or unconsciously to use the laws of nature for their individual benefit. They found that by thinking and planning they were not obliged to earn bread by hard manual labor, but could assume the relationship of employer to other men and have the work done by those who had not the faculty for planning and managing. In this manner there arose between men the relationship of employer and employé. Please do not understand me to say that the employer, the thinker, ceased working when he laid down his tools and became the manager of his own business, because I do not wish to be so understood. Cessation from work means retrogression; and retrogression soon becomes degeneration and stagnation. Stagnation whether it be spiritual, mental or material causes death. The great Consciousness Itself works during each Cosmic Day and each and every child of God who desires to progress must also work.

A great mistake most people make is in limiting the meaning of the word "work" to purely physical labor. Work does not necessarily mean physical effort. Man is mind, and mental strength and growth can come only through the exercise of his mental powers. The misapprehensions of the meaning of the Scriptural quotation, and of the laws of life and the law of opulence are due to the misconception of the meaning of the word "work."

Last year when these lectures were first delivered several persons said, "It is very wrong to teach that you can draw material things to yourself by the use of mental forces; you should teach that people must work for what they get."

It is obvious that these cautious souls have not developed beyond the physical plane and are unable to appreciate the fact that there may be mental as well as physical labor. Then there are other persons who do not desire to use Spiritual forces to draw to themselves material things and therefore protest against teaching this knowledge. It is quite reasonable to suppose that such persons find it difficult to manipulate spiritual forces and because they do not understand how to use them, they object to others using them. To such persons I have nothing to offer except good wishes for their progress along the lines of development they have chosen.

Man's evolution has enlarged the meaning of the word "work," and we now say, "In the sweat of thy face or through mental effort shalt thou earn bread." Employers, capitalists, and thinkers plan day after day and work very hard mentally, yet many of them never raise a hand to do physical labor, but leave that part of the work to be done by those persons who still believe they must earn bread in the sweat of their faces.

There are three classes of workers; first, the

physical workers; second, the physico-mental workers; and the third, or purely mental workers, and each of these classes marks a period of human evolution. By purely physical workers I mean the hewers of wood and the drawers of water—the mass of humanity. The physico-mental workers are those who, while recognizing that the laws of mind have a wonderful power to aid a man in his development and resources, use their minds for planning and enlarging their work and drawing Opulence to themselves and yet use physical means also for the purpose of manifesting it. The third class embraces all who are purely mental workers, those who have learned to use their minds along all lines and who use mental forces so fully and so completely that they receive whatever they desire without manual labor of any kind. These are conscious users of what is commonly called the Law of Opulence or the law which brings opulence. Some students call this the law of Demand and Supply. It really does not matter what it is called, it operates as unfailingly on the plane of mind as it does in the realm of economics.

Each person places himself in one of these three classes of workers, according to his evolutionary development. In the first mentioned class the law of opulence never manifests. Those who only work physically and individually can never acquire opulence. They earn a living, plus a little more than an actual living and that is all. The law of opulence commences to manifest in the second class, the physico-mental workers, and passes by slow gradation up through it to the third class where it manifests in its fullness. Every person in the course of his evolutionary career must pass through each of these three classes, and most persons who have reached our point of development are in the second class. This class is working with the laws of nature consciously while having a center through which to draw opulence. By a "center" I mean a certain definite vocation or avocation through which money comes. For example, suppose you have a small business—a news-stand perhaps. You have learned that there is such a thing as the law of mental demand and supply and you desire to use this law for your financial betterment. The small business is your center, and having a center you wish to enlarge it. You make a mental picture of a larger business and see yourself with a cigar and news-stand combined. You continue to look at that picture day after day and mentally demand that it shall be yours. If you never destroy your picture, in the course of time your demand will be met and the ways and means will be provided for you to get what you want. But you should not stop with the news-stand and cigar store combined, because it is never well to be content with a little. You should immediately go about making another picture, as soon as your demand has been met, and in this one you should see yourself supplying other newsstands; you should become a dealer and distributor.

Or perhaps you do not wish to have a newsstand. You may be engaged in another kind of business and are working for a salary. Perhaps you would like an advancement in your salary and a better position. Then you should make a mental picture of yourself occupying the position you want and drawing the salary you require, and by using this position for your center you will work upward and onward to any height you desire.

For illustration let us look at a woman who stood before the public as a teacher of metaphysics. I refer to Mrs. Mary Baker G. Eddy. She began her work as a practicing physician and after studying under Dr. Quimby learned that it was possible to make a practical application of the Berkeleyan philosophy for the purpose of healing the sick. She started with a very insignificant medical practice, which gradually grew to large proportions because of the remarkable cures she performed through mind. By the use of medicine and the knowledge that Dr. Quimby had given her, she proceeded to enlarge her center, to draw more people to her from different parts of the country, whom she healed and taught, receiving large sums of money for her services. Her center grew until, it is said, she died possessed of more than a million dollars.

If we do not like our occupation, there is no reason why we should continue to work at it forever; but we should hold the thought that we shall use it only for the present until we can draw to ourselves a better and a higher one. Faith in the law and the power of mind enables us to demonstrate over adverse financial conditions and make them what we desire.

A master of this art, whom I knew, was once a newsboy. Born of poor parents in one of the poorest quarters of Paris, he lived like all other children of his class in great destitution. His father and mother were rag-pickers and lived in a cellar. One day when he had reached the age of eighteen or twenty years a great Soul came into his life, and after engaging the boy to do some work for him became interested in his welfare, and commenced to teach him something about the power of mind. He also gave him a manuscript and told him to study and practice the teachings he would find therein.

The boy took the manuscript home and spent his last penny for a candle to give him light while he read about the Law of Demand and Supply; and as he read he began to believe that he could use this law to help himself out of his wretched condition. Looking around the tiny place which he called his bedroom, with its bare walls and stone floor, he said: "I shall commence now to create opulence for myself and the first thing I need to make me comfortable is a piece of carpet three feet long, that I can stand on while dressing when I get out of bed on cold mornings." He made the mental picture of the carpet and held steadily to his creation. After a while a piece of new carpet was given him by a woman whom he had served and from the moment his first demonstration was made, his faith in the law never wavered. He became a master at making demonstrations and when I first met him was possessed of a great many hundred thousand dollars.

Faith in something we cannot understand is hard to acquire and rarely amounts to anything more than a hope; but faith based upon immutable law grows to be knowledge. The small demonstrations made in the beginning of our work with the law are often the most important, because they prove to us that we have the power to put the law into operation.

In the class of the physico-mental workers we find the progressive student increasing his center and also attempting to make demonstrations independently of it. Such persons have made a marked advance in their evolutionary progress. For example, let us take the attorney who knows how to use the law of demand. He says, "I want a good law practice," and pictures clients coming in large numbers into his office. After a time the clients come as he has pictured, and then he begins to make a distinction between them. He says: "I want to represent only those whose cases I can win," and in this way he works for the mutual benefit of all who are interested. Then he begins to create things separate and distinct from his law practice. He wishes to go to Congress, perhaps, and makes a picture of himself representing his district at the Capitol, and after holding the picture for a while and earnestly making his demands that it shall come to him, an opportunity will be given and his pictures will materialize, because the law has been put into operation by his power of mind.

In the third class are those individuals who are able to draw to themselves whatever they desire irrespective of any center. Constant practice has made these persons skilled operators of the law and with them faith has grown into absolute knowledge. When a person has reached this point in his development he may go out of business and go wherever he desires because he can draw to himself anything he wants at any time or in any place he may happen to be. Many students pass through the second stage, that of the physico-mental workers, very slowly. A few pass rapidly since some have more faith than others, and after all it is largely a question of faith, for "Whatsoever a man thinketh in his heart so is he."

Mrs. Helen Wilmans-Post, the leader of the Mental Scientists, started, as you know, penniless in the world. She went to San Francisco with but a few dollars in her purse. When she arrived there she demanded and secured her first position on a newspaper, then she gradually drew to herself through that center money enough to enable her to live more comfortably than previously. After a while, in answer to her demands she got a better position. In the beginning she used the law of demand unconsciously—by following her own intuitions. Then she began to gain something of a knowledge of the working of the law and soon her brilliant career began as a conscious worker with the law. From a journalist she became an author, wrote several books and finally added healing and teaching to her long list of accomplishments. Through it all she continued to draw more and more opulence to herself until she was very rich. By her own example she has shown that she belongs to the second class of workers and makes the statement in her book, "The Conquest of Poverty," that no one can draw wealth to himself independently of physical effort.

Dr. Emily Cady is said to be a member of the third class. She has performed very remarkable

cures and has helped the world through her writings. Dr. Cady had used the law in healing and
her faith was great enough to believe she could
make other demonstrations of a more material nature. She passed into the third class it is said
when she showed her implicit faith in the law, by
demanding and receiving a large sum of money,
which she needed to reimburse herself for the time
and money she had given to suffering humanity.
She pictured the amount that she wanted and then
claimed it for her own and within a short time
after she made her creation, a stranger brought to
her what she had demanded. According to her
picture and her faith was it given unto her.

To put this law of opulence into operation it is
necessary to realize three things.

First. That everything you want exists now in
Divine Mind. Do you want jewels, gold, silver?
They are all in the market; besides, there are in
the mines as yet undiscovered all these things in
great abundance. All these things exist and you
can put into operation the law which will bring
them to you. The history of the world shows that
every mental demand of man has been met. Man
grew tired of walking and carrying things and the
cumbersome ox cart was evolved to supply his
needs. But he was not satisfied with this crude
vehicle and demanded something better. Then
came the horse and a lighter wagon, and after that

came steam cars, bicycles, and automobiles; and still man is not satisfied; he wishes to fly and flying machines are in the process of evolution. By degrees, from the boat made by burning out the center of an old log, has the modern steam yacht been evolved, and from the slow, tedious process of sending verbal messages by footmen from place to place has been evolved the wireless telegraph. There is no lack of anything in the world; and there should be no envy or jealousy between men, because there is enough of everything for everyone who lives.

Second. Realize that all things belong to Deity and that you can only have a temporary use of them. We should not be so vainglorious as to think we own anything. We came into the world destitute of everything and go out of it with nothing except character—and some even go without that. While we remain here we may borrow of Deity something or nothing according to our manner of thinking.

Third. We should realize that all things are distributed by the Universal Consciousness according to law. One man is not poverty-stricken and another man a millionaire by chance, fatalism or caprice; but everything is distributed according to the law of mental demand, or of asking and receiving. Those of you who are Christians know what the Nazarene said on that subject. Everyone who stops to think knows that the successful man of business has always been, is, and always will be, the man who can demand—i. e., make a positive picture of what he desires. If you want anything, create it mentally, demand it and according to your faith be it unto you.

There are certain rules whereby you may hasten your creations whether you work with or without a center, and your experiences will demonstrate the accuracy of the rules.

Rule First. Meditate and ask Deity if there is any reason why you should not have the thing you desire to create.

This removes all uncertainty from your mind about the advisability of creating it. Uncertainty produces a negative condition, disturbs your aura and therefore delays the materialization of your creations. When you have received the answer from the Universal Consciousness that it is right and proper for you to have the thing that you desire, you are then in a positive condition of mind and can forcefully put the law into operation.

Rule Second. Having decided to create something make your mental picture of it and demand it unfalteringly until it comes.

A person after having received a favorable answer from Deity often commences his creations, but abandons them after a time because his objective mind suggests that he may have been mistaken about his answer from Deity, and it is not best to continue with his demands. Do not listen to the suggestions from your objective mind, but once having decided upon your creations go on with them to the end.

Rule Three. A positive demand accomplishes more and better results than a request or a petition.

The mental attitude while making a demand should always be reverential but very positive. The Lord's Prayer is an excellent example of the proper attitude of mind to be assumed while demanding and we will analyze that prayer. Jesus said: "After this manner therefore pray ye:

"Our Father which art in Heaven, hallowed be Thy name. Thy Kingdom come. Thy will be done in earth, as it is in Heaven." The attitude of mind manifested by the Nazarene while making the first part of this prayer was reverential, and His words expressed His desire for perfect harmony between Himself and the Father. Having established harmony between His individual mind and the Universal Mind He proceeded to make His demands in this manner:

"*Give* us this day our daily bread: And *forgive* us our debts as we forgive our debtors. And *lead* us not into temptation, but *deliver* us from evil." After this manner therefore pray *ye*.

There is not one negative thought in this

prayer. There is a positive *demand* for everything desired rather than a petition. We can almost say that the demand was a respectful command that the things desired should come, and you will find that those of you who ask of the Universal in this manner and with this mental attitude will always receive what you ask for.

Now contrast the mental attitude that the Nazarene Occultist had when He prayed, with the mental attitude of His so-called followers of the present day. He said: ''When thou prayest thou shalt not be as the hypocrites are: for they love to pray standing (kneeling) in the synagogues'' (churches and cathedrals) * * * ''But when ye pray, use not vain repetitions as the heathen do; for they think that they shall be heard for their much speaking'' (chanting, litanies and masses). If you wish to witness the contrast between the Master's and the modern forms of worship, go into some of the Churches on or near Fifth Avenue and listen to the words of the modern prayers. On Sunday you will hear Public Confessions of sins something like this:

''We have left undone those things which we ought to have done; and we have done those things which we ought not to have done: And there is no health in us.'' ''Health'' is defined by the Century Dictionary as meaning in this connection, "natural vigor of the faculties, moral or intellectual soundness."

If we were to say about these same good citizens what they publicly admit about themselves—that they are morally and intellectually depraved and are secretly doing things they ought not to do— we should very likely be sued for slander. But we do not wish to say or to believe that these good people are guilty of what they unthinkingly say with their lips in their forms of worship. The illustration given is but a type of modern prayers, for they are all more or less self-depreciatory if not self-condemnatory. The thoughts behind them are negative and the prayers are repeated as a matter of form more than of faith. Many of these same good persons have their prayers answered, but the answered ones were not the formal prayers read from prayer books. They are those that were sent forth from the heart and were expressed in a positive form; they were whispered in the silence of the night when there was no one near to hear but God to whom they were addressed. These are the prayers that are efficacious, for prayer to be efficacious must be a mental and not an emotional act.

Rule Four. Demand specifically what you want.

Every word of this rule is important. First you must make a demand. Then that demand must be specific. Make your mental picture clear-cut.

The clearer your picture the sooner will it materialize. Demand specifically what you want—not what some one else wants you to have, not what you think you ought to have, not what you believe it your duty to want—but what you, yourself, wish to have.

The converse of this rule is equally important. Never demand what you do not want. If you want money do not demand work, but always be ready and willing to work for it—if necessary. Almost everyone in the beginning makes the mistake of demanding what he does not want, because it is difficult to break the customs of many years. Unpleasant environment is the result of demands we have made in the past for things we do not want now. Diseased bodies and unhappy conditions of mind are but the realizations of demands made in ignorance.

This rule is very likely to be misunderstood even by some metaphysicians. A local teacher of metaphysics who heard this rule given in last year's lectures said it was misleading; that if a person had a drug store, for instance, and wanted money, he should demand patrons because they would bring money. To an Occultist this is strange logic. The druggist might have a thousand patrons and sell his entire stock. If all his customers bought his goods on credit and neglected to pay for them afterwards, his desire for money would not be fulfilled although his demand for patrons had been fully met. It is best to demand the specific thing you want and then you will make no mistakes.

A member of last year's class who thought she understood this rule, said to me several weeks after the lecture course ended that she had created a trip to Europe. When I asked her to describe her mental picture she said, "Oh, I just created a one thousand dollar bill which I shall use for my trip." She had not created a trip to Europe, but had created the money to pay for one. This was no surety of her getting the trip, because when the money came an infinite number of things might occur to prevent her going. She should have created the picture of herself on board ship crossing the ocean; and should have seen herself landing safe and well on the other side.

Rule Fifth. Demand only when your desire is strong.

When you feel the need of a thing your desire for it is strongest. Many students begin enthusiastically to make their demands, but soon grow lukewarm. A good way to intensify your desires is to think of the pleasure the possession of the thing would give you, and when the desire for it comes sweeping over you then make your demand for it. Do not demand because the hour set apart for demanding has come, or because you regard it as a duty you have assumed. Demands made under such conditions amount to nothing, and the time put into work of that kind is wasted.

Rule Sixth. Mind works best when the body is still.

If you are drumming with your fingers or swinging your feet while making demands, a part of your mental force goes into the physical motions you are making; and your forces being divided the mental work is robbed of much of its power. You should conserve your force. At intervals during the day you may think of your demands and you can hold them subconsciously in mind much of the time; and while this kind of picture making does not accomplish as much as when the body is at rest, yet it does have an effect.

Rule Seventh. Never demand when excited.

You may have a strong desire but no excitement. A demand made during intense excitement is always met forcefully. This is an important rule, the observance of which may save you much inconvenience. We are quite likely to become impatient at times and are often tempted to make violent demands. It is a dangerous thing to do, as I shall show you in an illustration.

There was a student of Occultism in this city who had met with several misfortunes. Disasters followed each other till everything he had on the material plane was swept away. But he was possessed of a great deal of force, and knowing how to make demands for what he wanted he commenced making new creations. He demanded ten thousand dollars, which to him was financial opulence. The demand was not met immediately, and the young man became impatient and finally angry. And when he wakened one morning to find himself without money enough to pay for his breakfast, he walked to the park, threw himself upon the ground and lay there for several hours with his teeth set, hands clenched and with the perspiration standing out all over his body, so intense was his excitement while making his demand for the money he had pictured. The next day he boarded a freight train and, after the usual delays and inconveniences attending upon transportation of that kind, the student of Occultism managed to reach a Western town. But he had no sooner entered the place than a cyclone came along and swept it off the face of the earth. When the young man of the violent demands came to consciousness he was lying on the ground some distance from the place where he was at the last moment of his recollection. His body was a mass of bruises, and when he tried to rise to his feet he found one leg broken. Bodies of dead animals and men lay all around him, and wagonloads of débris were strewn in all directions; but just within reach of his arm lay a plethoric leather wallet. The young man reached his best arm out and got the wallet and immediately examined its contents. There were just ten one thousand dollar bills in it and not a scrap of paper or a card to tell to whom it belonged. He placed his prize in the pocket of his ragged coat and crept on his hands and knees for some distance till someone came to his relief. He was cared for and finally got well. The owner of the money could not be found, and the young man kept it as an answer to his violent demand, which so nearly cost him his life.

Please do not understand me to say that the young Occult student's violent demand created the cyclone, because it had nothing to do with its creation. But the student was drawn into the cyclone, and suffered the horrors of it, because of his own tempestuous mental condition when making a demand, which had to be met after the manner that it was made.

Rule Eighth. Always be deliberate and quiet but positive when demanding.

Never demand in a hurry. Mental perturbation engendered by hurry, delays the materialization of your creation.

Rule Ninth. Avoid speculating on the time when or the way in which your demonstrations will be made.

When you begin speculating about the ways and means by which your demonstrations will come, immediately your force becomes scattered or divided and a repellent expectancy arises. There is an expectancy that draws and also one that repels. The quiet expectancy, such as is used in meditation, is helpful in drawing to you whatever you have demanded. But the impatient expectancy of the objective mind is repellent, because it causes your aura to become disturbed and then nothing you want can reach you.

For example: You have made a demand and have commenced to wonder through whom that demand will be met. Your objective mind suggests Mr. Blank as the most probable person, and if you accept the suggestion when you meet Mr. Blank you are not mentally poised because of your impatient expectancy. Mr. Blank feels your mental condition and if he were inclined to form a business connection with you he would hesitate and become uncertain because of your perturbed condition; thus the ways and means that you expected to bring your demonstration would not be used because of your repellent expectancy. The person who violates rule nine is likely to make very bad investments.

Rule Tenth. Anger, discontent, envy and lack of self-control repel and delay a demonstration.

If you make a mental picture of a thing and hold it for a time it will materialize, but it will be delayed if you indulge in any of the mental attitudes just mentioned; because any of these puts your aura into a perturbed condition, which is repellent. Divine Mind may be likened to the ocean which is bearing a boat laden with your creations to you who are standing upon the shore. If you are perturbed your mind acts upon Divine Mind as the wind off shore acts upon the ocean. It is forever driving back the craft in which are the things you desire.

This rule is one of the hardest to observe, but like anything else it can be followed. It is the disregard of this rule which leads investigators and beginners to disbelieve in the law or power of mind, and which makes so many students finally abandon in despair their efforts to use the forces of nature. But if we do not use nature's forces then we shall be used by them.

Rule Eleventh. The earnestness with which a demand is made, the frequency with which it is made and the persistency with which the mental image is consciously held in mind hasten the demonstration.

In another lecture you were told how your mental picture becomes a matrix, and that from this matrix goes forth a vibratory force like a blue magnetic cord which connects with the thing you desire. The material thing is then drawn by this blue magnetic cord closer and closer to you every time you concentrate your thoughts upon your creation until the thing finally reaches you. The earnestness, the frequency and the persistency of your demands and concentration draw it faster and faster. An Occultist never destroys any of his mental pictures.

Rule Twelve. The realization that you are using an immutable law hastens your demonstrations.

Get out of the old theological belief that because you are good God is going to give you a reward. Get out of the thought that you are a chosen child of God and that He is looking upon you with special favor. Get into the thought that you are a student of Occultism and that by working with mental law you are going to be able to make quick demonstrations and a better environment. Realize that you are using an immutable law and that what you demand comes to you because you are using a law and that nothing can prevent its coming, that God Himself cannot prevent it without violating His own nature—a thing inconceivable.

Rule Thirteen. After your creation is made and you have demanded it, the declaration, "God has met my demand," hastens the material manifestation of the demonstration.

For example, suppose you have made a picture, have held it, have demanded that it should materialize and you have followed faithfully all the foregoing rules. But after a while your objective mind says: "That demonstration will never come." Then I would suggest that you change your form of demand, and instead of saying "Give me this," say, "God has met my demand. It is mine now." Claim it. You know your demand has been met on the mental plane, and since it is law that you are using, it is yours as much before it has materialized as it will be afterward. This declaration gives you a positive realization of possession which has a tendency to bring more quickly your creations and removes anxiety and perturbation from your mind.

If this lecture on opulence has been made clear, you will understand that I am not teaching a *mental-get-rich-quick* affair, nor the getting of something for nothing; but that you must work mentally in order to accomplish whatever you desire. The particular advantage of this system of mental work over physical work is this: you can select your own time to do it, and arrange your own compensation. The results are absolutely certain if the law is complied with. But when a person says he has complied with the rules given here and has not got results he has made a mistake somewhere. He has not complied.

Your experiences with prosperous business men and all successful persons in the world show that unconsciously they work along these lines. I say unconsciously because the majority of them as yet only unconsciously put the law into operation. Observation of the metaphysicians of the present day who are semi-consciously using the law—and their name is legion—will show that even with their limited knowledge they are repeatedly making remarkable demonstrations. A large per cent of those who listened to these lectures last season have been enabled to demonstrate health for themselves and many have brought health to others; some have demonstrated happiness, others have enlarged their business and many have drawn to themselves money. All have increased their store of knowledge and a few have become ennobled in character and have gained spiritual qualities. This shows that the law has worked on the three planes of being with this band of students and if a few can accomplish many can.

If you will but persist in your faith there can be no limit to your possibilities. If you can demonstrate a piece of carpet three feet long you can demonstrate a million dollars. If you can cure a headache you can cure in the course of time any disease; if you can demonstrate a seat in the street car you can demonstrate a seat in Congress, in time. If you can be happy a week you can be happy for a lifetime, because what can be done in a small degree can, with persistency, be done in a large degree.

It rests with you whether you will or will not

use this law consciously. There are some of you who will. There is always a percentage of persons who succeed and a percentage who do not. Each of you can do with your knowledge what you choose. This much is true, if you persist for two years to consciously use these laws in your daily affairs of life, by the end of that time your environment will have changed sufficiently, and demonstrations enough will have been made, to prove to you that you are dealing with *Law*.

INDEX

INDEX

Accidents, none in the World, 276

Acids, Mind in Action Creates, 259

Adamic Curse, 278

Adepts, 10, 15, 18; Aid Men, 19, 60; as Teachers, 10, 15, 196; Custodians of Occult Sciences, 11

Affinity, Chemical, a Form of Consciousness, 28, 88; Sex desire manifests as in Minerals, 87

Affirmations in Disease, 266, 267, 268, 273

Ages of Earth, 12-18; Fifth, Present One, 12, 17, 18; First, 12; Fourth, 14-17; Second, 12; Sun Cycles Determine, 103; Third, 13, 14

Aggrandizement, Individual, 246

Altruism, Cause of, 249; Force Dissipated in, 249; Green Force Antidote for, 248, 249; versus Selfishness, 9, 41

America, Ancient Civilization, 16, 17

Anesthetics, Man Is Mind Proved by, 55; Mind is Not Product of Brain Proved by, 55

Anger Caused by Fear, 83; Causes Congestion, 259; Color of, 147, 148, 244

Anger, Control of Others Necessitates Elimination of, 76; Demagnetizes Atoms of Body, 243, 244; Effect on Self-Control, 77; Red Color of, 147, 242, 244; Repels Demonstrations, 299, 300

Animal Kingdom, Consciousness in, 29, 67, 68; Independence in, 277; Re-embodiment in, 107-110; Souls in, 183; Vegetable Kingdom Supports, 264

Animal Propensities, Color of, 139

Animals, Blue Force Cannot be Used by, 250; Orange Force Used in Treatment of, 245

Answers to Demands, 158-163; Rules to Test, 162, 163

Anthropomorphism, 27

Apollonius of Tyana, Cosmic Forces Used by, 236

Art, Blue Force Inspires, 250, 251

Asceticism, Moral Reaction from Sensuousness, 86; Spirituality Not Gained by, 86, 87

Assyria, 18

Astrology, Revival of, 8

Atlantis, History of, 14, 15; Misuse of Suggestion Destroyed, 216; Occultism Openly Taught in, 15

Atlas, Altruist Desires to Become an, 249

Atoms, Anger Demagnetizes, 243, 244; Conscious Side of, 63; Dual Nature of, 35

Atonement, 90

Atrophy of Body Not Taught, 88

in Control of, 76-80, 91, 92;
Sensuousness an (see Sensuousness), 82, 86, 88; Sex
Desire an (see Sex Desire),
82, 87; Subjective Mind Can
Control, 91, 92; Vanity an,
(see Vanity), 82, 88-91
Emotion, Conquering of, Aids
in, 82, 92-99; Law of Periodicity Helps in, 93-96; Suggestions Used in, 96, 98;
Thinking With Subjective
Mind Helps in, 91; Will
Must Be Exercised in, 91
Entities on Subjective Side of
Life, 180, 183-186; Pose as
Teachers, 195
Environment—Shows Which
Consciousness Controls, 72;
Thoughts Determine, 118-122
Envy Repels Demonstrations,
299, 300
Epilepsy, Mental Treatment of,
189, 190, 269; Obsession
Causes, 189
Equilibrium, Law of (see Justice, Law of).
Esotericism, Jesus Taught, 4;
Teachings of, 2, 5, 6; Teachings for Students, 4
Essence, Divine. See Deity
Essenes, Cosmic Forces Used
by, 236
Eternity, Length of, 99
Ether—Birth of Minds from,
62-64; Defined, 37, 38, 39;
Nature of, 38-43
Everything, Ability to do, Can
Be Gained, 2, 174; Belongs to
Deity, 289; Distributed by
Law, 289, 290; Enough of
for Everybody, 289; Exists
in Deity, 6; Is Unfoldment
of Deity, 6; Law Governs,
119, 276, 279, 299; Must Unfold, 2; Temporary Use of,
289
Evil, Creation of Objective

Mind, 73, 74; Result of Ignorance, 72, 74, 93, 108
Evolution—As Divine Energy
or Impulse, 6; Centers of
Consciousness Necessary for,
39, 59; Dissolution Alternates With, 99; Occultism
Teaches, 6; Of Soul, 20; Of
Universe, 99-101; Process of,
3, 5, 59-61, 114; Works
Through Individuals, 59
Excitement of on Demands,
295-297
Exotericism, Jesus Taught, 4,
5; Masses Are Taught, 4
Eyesight Failing, How to Cure,
249

Fa, Corresponds to Green
Force, 247; Keynote of Earth,
247
Failures Caused by Fear, 70,
71, 83, 145
Fairies Are Elementals, 180
Faith, According to, Be It
Unto You, 290, 304; Assists
in Conquering Circumstances,
283; Based Upon Ignorance
Only a Hope, 285; Based
Upon Law, Becomes Knowledge, 285; Curers, Healing
by, Based on Law, 236; Salvation Does Not Depend
Upon, Alone, 64
Fear. See Emotion, Conquering of; Acquired Before
Birth, 70; Acquirement of
Objective Mind, 70, 71; Analyzed, 83; Base of Most Anger, Jealousy, Murder, Failure, Theft, Discouragement,
Despondency, 83; Basic Emotion, 82, 83; Causes Cancer,
71; Causes Failures, 70, 71,
83, 144, 145; Causes Fevers,
259; Causes Heart Troubles,
259; Color of, 144, 244; Control of, 83-86, 91-98; Creates

COSIMO is a specialty publisher of books and publications that inspire, inform and engage readers. Our mission is to offer unique books to niche audiences around the world.

COSIMO CLASSICS offers a collection of distinctive titles by the great authors and thinkers throughout the ages. At COSIMO CLASSICS timeless classics find a new life as affordable books, covering a variety of subjects including: *Biographies, Business, History, Mythology, Personal Development, Philosophy, Religion and Spirituality*, and much more!

COSIMO-on-DEMAND publishes books and publications for innovative authors, non-profit organizations and businesses. COSIMO-on-DEMAND specializes in bringing books back into print, publishing new books quickly and effectively, and making these publications available to readers around the world.

COSIMO REPORTS publishes public reports that affect your world: from global trends to the economy, and from health to geo-politics.

FOR MORE INFORMATION CONTACT US AT
INFO@COSIMOBOOKS.COM

If you are a book-lover interested in our current catalog of books.

If you are an author who wants to get published

If you represent an organization or business seeking to reach your members, donors or customers with your own books and publications

**COSIMO BOOKS ARE ALWAYS
AVAILABLE AT ONLINE BOOKSTORES**

——————— VISIT COSIMOBOOKS.COM ———————
BE INSPIRED, BE INFORMED